THE

EVERYTHING

WEDDING
ORGANIZER

The Everything Wedding Series:

The Everything® Jewish Wedding Book
The Everything® Wedding Book
The Everything® Wedding Checklist
The Everything® Wedding Etiquette Book
The Everything® Wedding Vows Book
The Everything® Wedding Organizer

THE

EVERYTHING

WEDDING ORGANIZER

**Checklists, calendars,
and worksheets for planning
the perfect wedding**

Laura Morin

Adams Media Corporation
Holbrook, Massachusetts

An Everything® Series Book. The Everything® Series
is a registered trademark of Adams Media Corporation.

Published by Adams Media Corporation
260 Center Street, Holbrook, MA 02343

ISBN: 1-55850-828-7

Printed in Korea.

J I H G F E

This publication is designed to provide accurate and authoritative information with
regard to the subject matter covered. It is sold with the understanding that the
publisher is not engaged in rendering legal, accounting, or other professional
advice. If legal advice or other expert assistance is required, the services of a
competent professional person should be sought.
  —From a *Declaration of Principles* jointly adopted by a Committee of the
American Bar Association and a Committee of Publishers and Associations

Illustrations by Barry Littmann and Joanna Hodgens.

This book is available at quantity discounts for bulk purchases.
For information, call 1-800-872-5627 (in Massachusetts, call 781-767-8100).

Visit our home page at http://www.adamsmedia.com

Contents

PART ONE: GETTING STARTED

Chapter 1: Your Engagement

Chapter 2: Resolving "Big Picture" Issues

Chapter 3: Your Wedding Style

PART TWO: THE WEDDING CEREMONY

Chapter 8: Planning Your Wedding Ceremony

Chapter 9: Making It Official

Chapter 10: Style for the Aisle

PART THREE: THE RECEPTION

Chapter 11: Planning Your Wedding Reception

Chapter 12: Wedding Photography and Videography

Chapter 17: Wedding Transportation

PART FOUR: INTO THE SUNSET

Chapter 18: Planning Your Honeymoon

Chapter 19: Last-Minute Details

Acknowledgments

This book would not have been possible without the prior efforts of Sharon Capen Cook, Elizabeth Gale, Janet Anastasio, Michelle Bevilacqua, and Emily Ehrenstein. I applaud them all for their hard work, humor, and creativity. Thanks also to Pam Liflander who, in addition to being a talented editor, is a good friend.

Introduction

Congratulations! You've decided to get married. Once the shock begins to wear off, you're probably going to have a lot of questions about the whole wedding process—not to mention a lot to do! But don't worry, this book is designed to help you make planning your wedding as easy and stress-free as possible. Who knows? You might even enjoy it!

In order to get you to the big day in one piece, we've broken down the overwhelming task of planning a wedding into small, simple steps. We've included worksheets, planning calendars, budget planners, charts, and checklists so you can keep all the essential information in one easy-to-use handbook. And its convenient size means you can take it with you to the many appointments you will have over the next few months, so you'll have all the dates, names, and addresses you need right at your fingertips! Feeling nervous? Don't. Just keep this book handy and you'll have everything covered.

Good luck!

GETTING
STARTED

PART ONE

GETTING STARTED

CHAPTER ONE

YOUR ENGAGEMENT

Announcement Protocol

Once you've made the big decision, you'll probably want to tell everyone you know—and even people you don't. But wait! As excited as you may be, calm down, collect yourself, and think about who should be told first. There is a certain protocol that should be followed, and you don't want to offend anyone. (Unfortunately, bowing to protocol is something you're going to have to get used to. Unless you truly feel comfortable throwing courtesy and tradition to the wind, these are usually as big a part of planning and having a wedding as your budget, your gown, and your guest list.)

Telling Your Family and Friends

Announce your engagement in person to both sets of parents. It's up to you and your fiancé to decide whether to tell your own parents privately or make the announcement together. If either your or his parents live too far away for you to do so, call them to pass on the good news. If possible, try to arrange a visit soon afterwards so that everyone can start getting acquainted (if they haven't already). Discuss the possibility of getting all the future in-laws together before the wedding.

If either you or your groom has children from a previous marriage, make sure that they are told of the impending new marriage right away; don't let them hear it from someone else! A parent's new marriage can be a stressful event for children. Give them all the reassurance they need, try to sense and quell their fears, and make them as much a part of the wedding as the situation allows.

After you've told your respective families, it's time to start yelling the news from the rooftops. Tell your friends and coworkers. If you've already selected your attendants, you may want to ask them to be in your wedding at the time you announce your engagement. Or you may ask them later on, perhaps after you've set the wedding date.

Newspaper Announcements

One easy and time-tested way to spread the word of your impending nuptials is via a newspaper announcement. This announcement is usually made by the parents of the bride, not more than one year prior to the wedding. Typically, it gives the names of the bride and groom, their parents' names, and the wedding date. Many couples include an official engagement photo along with the announcement, or a photo of the bride alone. (For more information on engagement photos, see the chapter on wedding photography and videography.)

The announcement information is usually sent to the lifestyle or society editor of your local newspaper, but you might want to call the paper's offices just to make sure. You should also inquire about any fees you may be charged; this is a common practice these days, arising from the abundance of marriage notices many papers receive.

If the groom's family lives in another city or state, be sure to send them a copy of a photo and the newspaper announcement worksheet that appears in this chapter, so they can arrange for an announcement in their local paper as well.

If you're planning a very long engagement (one year or more), you may want to wait a while before sending an announcement to the newspaper, as they are usually printed no earlier than a year before the wedding.

Here is an example of a standard announcement:

Mr. and Mrs. George T. Barker of Boston, Massachusetts, announce the engagement of their daughter Melissa Ann to Jeffrey Martin, son of Mr. and Mrs. Wayne B. Martin of Cambridge, Massachusetts. A June wedding is planned.

If your parents are divorced, the announcement is typically made by the parent with whom you live; the other parent is mentioned (*Ms. Barker is also the daughter of* . . .). Alternatively, the divorced parents may choose to make the announcement together (*Mr. George T. Barker of New York City and Ms. Ellen Weiss of Boston announce* . . .). A deceased parent is announced as "the late Mr. Barker."

Newspaper Engagement Announcement Worksheet

To appear in _____ newspaper on _____ (date).

Names of the bride's parents: _____

_____

Address: _____

_____

Telephone number with area code: _____

Mr. and Mrs. _____ of _____ announce the
                  (bride's parents' names)   _(their city, if out of town)_

engagement of their daughter, _____, to _____ ,
                    (bride's first and middle names) _(groom's first and last names)_

the son of Mr. and Mrs. _____ , of _____ .
                (groom's parents' names)   _(groom's parents' city)_

A _____ wedding is planned. (Or, No date has been set for the wedding.)
(month/season)

Engagement Parties

Although the family of the bride usually hosts some sort of an engagement party, it's perfectly acceptable for the family of the groom (or anyone else) to host such an affair, particularly if the bride's family lives far away. Most engagement parties are very informal, with invites made via phone or a handwritten note. The party is usually held either at the host's home or in a restaurant.

The only hint of formality at an engagement party is the toast made by the father of the bride to the couple. This is usually followed by a responding toast from the groom. Anyone else wishing to offer a toast may then do so. When all the toasting is finished, it's on to the celebrating, which is, of course, only a minor version of the big celebration to come: your wedding.

Show your appreciation by sending a thank-you note and perhaps a small gift to the hosts of any parties given in honor of you and your fiancé. Also be sure you also send a prompt thank-you note to anyone who gives you an engagement gift.

Finding a Reputable Jeweler

Odds are that, by the time you look at this, you'll already be able to read by the glare of your diamond engagement ring. Okay, maybe that's a bit of an exaggeration, but it is true that most brides-to-be these days have their engagement ring before they publicly announce their betrothal—and start looking through books like this to help them plan the wedding. Even if you're part of this majority, you might find this section informative and even useful, especially if you're considering purchasing diamond wedding bands.

Before you and your fiancé even start to consider purchasing rings from a jewelry store, determine the budget you have to work with. As a general rule, spend no more than three weeks' salary or 6 percent of your income on each ring. Yes, you want good-quality rings that will stand the test of time, but by the same token, you don't want to still be paying for them when your twenty-fifth wedding anniversary rolls around. These are rough guidelines, of course; if you have more to spend, by all means, go ahead. Conversely, if 6 percent of your salary seems a bit steep, go with a price range that is more appropriate for you.

The best way to find a reputable jeweler is by referral. Ask your friends and family about the jewelers they've used. If no one has any suggestions, the next best thing is to pick a store that appeals to you, appears to stock jewelry in your price range, and is a member of the American Gem Society. Members of the AGS must meet high standards of quality and reputability, so when you choose one of these stores, you know you'll be getting the best—and you won't be getting taken.

Jewelry Shopping Tips

- Shop around. Even if you fall in love with a ring at the first store you visit, it pays to get some perspective by comparing selections from other jewelers. Remember, you can always return to the first store. Beware of shops that pressure you to buy on the spot.
- Don't hesitate to ask if the price is negotiable; it almost always is.
- Make the final sale contingent upon your taking the ring to an appraiser of your choice to verify value and price. Some jewelers will try to dupe you into buying a ring for much more than it's worth by having their appraiser (or one they recommend) "confirm" the ring's inflated value.
- Before handing over any cash, get a purchase agreement that includes stipulations for sizing and potential return. Does the store offer a money-back guarantee if the ring is

returned within the designated time frame? Any sizing, tightening, or cleaning required during the first six months of ownership should be free.

🌸 Get a written appraisal that describes the ring and cites its value for insurance purposes.

🌸 Insure your rings under your homeowner's or renter's policy.

Selecting Your Engagement and Wedding Rings

A diamond ring is the most popular kind of engagement ring. There are four guidelines to go by when judging the quality of a diamond: clarity, cut, color, and carat, also known as the "Four C's." The diamond you or your fiancé purchases should pass the test in each of these categories.

CLARITY

The clarity of a diamond is measured by the number of its flaws or imperfections (either interior or exterior). Clarity, broadly speaking, is the most important factor in determining the beauty of a given stone: a stone with low clarity, for example, will have a number of imperfections when viewed under a gemologist's magnifying glass.

CUT

The cut of a diamond is the stone's physical configuration, the result of the process whereby the rough gem is shaped. The diamonds you will be shown by a jeweler have had many cuts made on the surface of the stone to shape them and emphasize their brilliance. Common shapes include the "round" (or "brilliant"), pear-shaped, oval, and marquise cuts.

Round   *Oval*   *Pear*   *Marquise*   *Emerald*

COLOR

The color of the diamond is also a major factor in determining its value. Stones that are colorless are considered to be perfect. The object, then, is to find a stone that is as close to colorless as possible—unless, of course, your personal preference dictates otherwise. (Many people prefer to wear stones with a slight discoloration, even though these stones are not—financially, at any rate—worth as much as higher-quality diamonds.)

CARAT

The diamond's carat weight refers to the actual size of the stone. (Unlike the carat weight of gold, the carat weight of a diamond is simply a physical measure of the weight of the item in question—and not a measure of quality or purity.) Bear in mind that carat weight alone is not necessarily an indicator of price or value. A three-quarter-carat weight, colorless, flawless diamond will almost certainly be appraised higher than a two-carat weight stone with several flaws and a murky, yellowish tint.

After the stone is selected, it's time to think about the ring you're going to attach it to. Most people choose to go with a yellow gold ring, although white gold, platinum, and silver are options. How do you judge the value of a gold band? Generally by carat weight and appearance. As mentioned above, the term carat does tell you something about purity when it's applied to gold. The carat system designates how many parts out of 24 are pure gold in a given piece of jewelry. (Since gold is such a soft metal, it is sometimes blended with another, stronger metal.) Therefore, a ring that is 18-carat gold is three-quarters pure. While it may be tempting to choose "pure" gold, gold strengthened with another metal is much more durable. This is why jewelry made of 18-carat gold is generally more wear-resistant than that made of 24-carat gold.

The way the diamond (or any other stone) is placed on the band is known as the setting. Some rings are set high, away from the band, meaning that more of the stone is exposed; others are set low. Before you decide on a setting, consider the everyday treatment your ring will get. If you work with your hands, or are often in an environment where you're likely to knock your ring finger against something and scratch or dislodge the stone—architects, engineers, schoolteachers, nurses, and hairdressers beware—you might want to have your ring set low. However, a higher setting means more light can get under the stone, making for a more brilliant appearance.

WEDDING BANDS

Many couples today wear matching wedding bands. There's no rule to that effect, however, so you and your fiancé should feel free to choose bands that suit each of your tastes. Sometimes the bride will buy her band as part of a matched set with her engagement ring. If you don't buy such a set, the band you purchase should complement your engagement ring. If you don't have an engagement ring, you may prefer a diamond wedding band over a plain one.

Many couples choose to have the inside of their bands engraved, usually with the date of the wedding and their future spouse's name or initials.

While etiquette dictates that you pay for the groom's band and he pay for yours, the two of you should feel free to buck this rule and work out whatever arrangement you see fit.

You should order your wedding bands three to six months before the wedding. This will give you plenty of time to make sure the rings are fitted properly.

Jewelry store #1: _____

Address: _____

Telephone number: _____

Sales representative: _____

Store hours: _____

Notes: _____

_____

_____

ℰℯ ℰℯ ℰℯ

Jewelry store #2: _____

Address: _____

Telephone number: _____

Sales representative: _____

Store hours: _____

Notes: _____

_____

_____

ℰℯ ℰℯ ℰℯ

Jewelry store #3: _____

Address: _____

Telephone number: _____

Sales representative: _____

Store hours: _____

Notes: _____

_____

_____

_____

Stone	#1	#2	#3	#4	#5
Jewelry store					
Clarity					
Cut					
Color					
Carats					
Other stones (if applicable)					
Setting					
Notes					
Price per carat					
Tax, other charges					
Total price					

Final choice: _____ Ring size: _____

  (stone number from above)

Order date: _____ Date ready: _____

Deposit amount: _____ Due date: _____

Balance: _____ Due date: _____

Notes: _____

_____

_____

_____

_____

	Bride's wedding band	Groom's wedding band	Other jewelry (if applicable)
Jewelry store			
Description			
Setting			
Stones (if applicable)			
Notes			
Price			
Tax, other charges			
Total price			

CHAPTER TWO

RESOLVING "BIG PICTURE" ISSUES

Setting the Date

When people learn of your engagement, the first thing you're likely to hear after "Congratulations!" is. "When's the date?" Until you set a date, you will have no good answer to this question, and even worse, you will be unable to go ahead with any of your other planning. Knowing the date is absolutely crucial. Without it, you have no accurate idea of when you will need the ceremony and reception sites; how long you have to find a dress; when you will need a photographer, a caterer, a florist, or any of the other professionals whose time you will be paying for; or even what colors and what types of flowers would look best in that season. A great deal is riding on the date you choose, so unless you don't really care about who, what, when, where, and how your wedding takes place, give the options some careful consideration and then select a date you can stick to.

In choosing a date, ask yourself: What season do you prefer? Do you want a country garden wedding in the spring? A seaport wedding in the summer? A celebration at a refurbished farmhouse in the fall? Does the season matter to you at all? If not, is there a time of year that your family or the groom's family will find particularly meaningful? Once you get an idea of the time of year you want, you can get started working on the details.

How much time do you have to plan the wedding? Does the availability of a ceremony and reception site coincide with your desired date? Are there any conflicts that exist for you, your family, or potential attendants (such as another wedding, a vacation, a graduation, or a pregnancy/birth)? It's doubtful your matron of honor would enjoy standing beside you in her eighth month in a dress that could double for a tent. By the same token, your parents are unlikely to appreciate having to choose between attending your wedding and your brother's high school graduation.

Are there military commitments to consider? If either you or your fiancé is in the military, you must work out an appropriate time to take leave. The same is to be considered if there is a close relative or special friend in the military who wishes to be there for your big day.

How many other couples will be getting married around the same time? The peak season for weddings is between April and October, so there may be a lot of competition out there for everything from flowers to frosting. You may want to consider having your wedding in the "off-season."

Should you have your wedding on a holiday weekend, such as Memorial Day, Labor Day, or Columbus Day? There are pros and cons to this idea. On the plus side, people may appreciate a wedding on a long weekend; it gives them an extra day to recuperate from the festivities, or to travel if they are coming from another city or state. For you and your fiancé, taking your honeymoon during a holiday week may give you an extra day away (or allow you to save a vacation day for a later time). But what if your guests have some long weekend vacation plans of their own? All these are factors to consider.

The most popular months for weddings are August, June, and September. December is also a popular wedding month, most likely because of the festive air and beautiful decorations of the Christmas season. The most popular days are Saturday, Friday, and Sunday. The most popular hours for the ceremony are 11:00 a.m., 2:00 p.m., and 4:00 p.m.

Creating a Master Plan

Once the initial surprise and excitement of the engagement has subsided, it is time to settle down, put your nose to the grindstone, and, like a field general, start mapping out a battle plan for your wedding. Make no mistake about it, planning your wedding will be a battle: a battle to get everything as coordinated, beautiful, on time, and generally perfect as your most important day should be. It's often a challenge, but take heart; if you go about it the right way, you will get it all done. Occasionally, you may feel it's all too big for you to handle. When that happens, stop, take a breath, and remember that once you start your walk down the aisle, it will all be worth it.

First, make up a schedule and stick to it. Though your tendency may be to procrastinate in the early months, don't! Don't worry, you won't be bored later; there will be plenty to do as the wedding draws near. Wouldn't you rather be free to deal with new issues, instead of being bogged down by tasks that could have been done months ago? Sticking to your schedule is the best and only way to make things go smoothly.

Plan to secure the key items in your wedding (ceremony site, reception site, caterer, photographer, flowers, gown, rings, music) as far in advance as possible. Starting early gives you the breathing room to take your time and make unrushed choices.

In-laws and Outlaws

When planning a wedding, one possible source of tension can come from the groom's family. Though the bride's family is traditionally in charge of the majority of the wedding details, this can sometimes make the groom's family feel left out, or as if they are being ordered around without consideration. Sometimes there is also competition between future mothers-in-law, each tending to baby her child, each wanting to have a hand in everything.

To avoid potential teeth gnashing whenever the families meet, keep the groom's family informed of all the wedding details, and consult with them on all major decisions. Have the mother in charge consult with the other mother to make the latter feel important and included.

For your part, be patient and, most of all, diplomatic. As hard (and embarrassing) as it may be, speak openly and honestly and confront potential problems in advance, so that when the wedding day comes, you and your groom need only be concerned with having the time of your lives.

Determining Your Budget

Is money no object when it comes to your wedding? Are you one of the very few (and very lucky) people who has an unlimited supply of funds just waiting to be spent on the wedding of a lifetime? Great! Skip the rest of this chapter. Go all out and make your wedding the extravaganza of your dreams.

If you're like most people these days, though, you'll need to set up a budget. If money is especially tight, it's best to prioritize so that your wedding can have the things that are most important to you.

First, decide on the kind of wedding you want. Your job will be to try to construct a budget based on that, using the resources available to you. Perhaps you and your fiancé don't even want a "big" formal (or semiformal) wedding. You may both shy away from frills and thrills, preferring to avoid much of the headaches and expense by holding a small, simple affair. If this is how you want to go, there are plenty of options: a backyard wedding, a wedding in a home, a civil ceremony—it's up to the two of you. Budgeting such a wedding should be fairly simple. You may decide, though, that you want as much of the grand, traditional wedding that your budget will allow. In this case, planning your expenses becomes particularly important. You'll want to make every dollar go as far as it possibly can. (See Chapter 3 for more on how to decide what kind of wedding you want.)

After you decide on the kind of wedding you'd like to have, you'll need to figure out exactly how you're going to afford it. The amounts you allocate yourself will help you determine the number of guests you can invite, the location of your reception, the food you will serve, the number of photographs you will have taken, the flowers on display, and many other elements of the celebration.

Who Pays for What

The best way to arrive at your budget is to determine what amount of money all of the parties involved—bride, groom, bride's parents, and groom's parents—can and/or will contribute. As the section below indicates, it is customary for the bride's family to bear the majority of the wedding expenses, but circumstances can dictate other arrangements. These days it is not uncommon for the bride and groom to bear the brunt of the wedding expenses themselves.

The bride and her family traditionally pay for . . .

- The groom's wedding ring and gift
- Invitations, reception cards, and announcements
- The bride's wedding gown and accessories
- The fee for the ceremony location
- Flowers for ceremony and reception (including flowers for the attendants)
- Housing for the bridesmaids
- Gifts for the bridesmaids
- Photography
- Music for ceremony and reception
- Any rented transportation, such as limousines
- All reception costs (location rental, food, decorations, etc.)

The groom and his family traditionally pay for . . .

- The bride's wedding and engagement rings
- A gift for the bride
- Housing for the ushers
- The marriage license
- The officiant's fee
- The bride's bouquet
- The bride's going-away corsage (optional)
- Mothers' and grandmothers' corsages
- Boutonnieres for groom's wedding party
- The rehearsal dinner
- The honeymoon

The maid/matron of honor and bridesmaids traditionally pay for . . .

- Their dresses and accessories
- A gift for the couple
- A shower gift
- A contribution to the bridal shower
- Transportation to and from the wedding

The best man and ushers traditionally pay for . . .

🌸 Their clothing rental (tuxedo, suit)
🌸 A gift for the couple
🌸 A contribution to the cost of the bachelor party
🌸 Transportation to and from the wedding

Remember, these guidelines are not set in stone. No one will faint or put out a warrant for your arrest if your family, instead of the groom's, hosts the rehearsal dinner, or if the groom pays for the photography. If circumstances require doing things differently, don't let these guidelines stop you.

There are many compromises you can make that will have little or no effect on your or your guests' enjoyment of the day. You may opt to get your invitations done by an offset printer instead of having them engraved, have a DJ instead of a band, or hold a buffet instead of a sit-down dinner. The goal is to prioritize so you can spend money on what is most important to you, on the things you are most likely to remember in the future.

Tipping Guidelines

Even the most budget-conscious brides and grooms often overlook one very substantial expense—tips! Depending on the size of your reception and your reception location, tipping can easily add from a few hundred to a few thousand dollars to your costs. Many wedding professionals even include a gratuity in their contract, and then expect an additional tip at the reception. As a result, whom to tip and how much to tip can often be perplexing dilemmas. Although tipping is, for the most part, expected, it is never required—it's simply an extra reward for extraordinary service. Exactly how much or whom you tip is completely at your discretion. The following are simply guidelines, not rules:

🌸 Caterers and reception site managers usually have gratuities of 15–20 percent included in their contracts. These are usually paid in advance by the host of the reception. If the caterer or manager has been exceptionally helpful, you may

wish to give him or her an additional tip, usually $1–$2 per guest.

🌸 Wait staff usually receive 15–20 percent of the food bill. Caterers sometimes include this gratuity in their contract. But if the tip is not included, give the tip to the head waiter or maitre d' during the reception.

🌸 Bartenders should be tipped 15–20 percent of the total bar bill. If their gratuity is already included in the catering contract, an additional tip of 10 percent is common. It should be paid by the host during the reception. Don't allow the bartender to accept tips from guests; ask him to put up a small sign that says, "No tipping, please."

🌸 Restroom, coat check, or parking attendants should be pre-paid by the host, usually $1–$2 per guest or car. Ask the staff not to accept tips from guests.

🌸 Limousine drivers usually receive 15–20 percent of the bill. Any additional tips are at the host's discretion.

🌸 Musicians or DJs may be tipped if their performance was exceptional. Tips usually run about $25 per band member. DJs are tipped about 15–20 percent of their fee.

🌸 Florists, photographers, and bakers are not usually tipped; you simply pay a flat fee for their services.

🌸 An officiant is never tipped; he or she receivers a flat fee for performing the service. A religious officiant may ask for a small donation, around $20, for his or her house of worship, but a civil officiant is not allowed to accept tips.

Should You Hire a Wedding Consultant?

Professional wedding planners may not have quite the same recognition as professional athletes and entertainers, but to many harried brides, they are truly superstars. Otherwise known as wedding consultants, these walking wedding encyclopedias will have the answers to all your questions, or will at least know where to find answers. You'll pay for the expertise, of course—but if your schedule is a hectic one, you may come to the conclusion that it's worth it.

Name:

Address:

Phone:

Contact:

Hours:

ஃ ஃ ஃ

Appointments:

Date: Time:

Date: Time:

Date: Time:

Date: Time:

ஃ ஃ ஃ

Service:

Number of hours:

Overtime cost:

Provides the following services:

Cost:

Fee: ❑ Flat   ❑ Hourly percentage: _____   ❑ Per guest

Total amount due: _____

Amount of deposit: _____ Date: _____

Amount due: _____ Date: _____

Gratuities included?   ❑ Yes   ❑ No

Sales tax included?   ❑ Yes   ❑ No

Date contract signed: _____

Terms of cancellation: _____

_____

_____

_____

_____

Notes: _____

_____

_____

_____

_____

_____

_____

_____

_____

_____

_____

Wedding Budget Worksheet

Item	Projected Cost (including tax, if applicable)	Deposit Paid	Balance Due	Who Pays?
WEDDING CONSULTANT				
Fee				
Tip (usually 15–20%)				
PREWEDDING PARTIES				
Engagement (if hosted by bride and groom)				
Site rental				
Equipment rental				
Invitations				
Food				
Beverages				
Decorations				
Flowers				
Party favors				
Bridesmaids' party/luncheon				
Rehearsal dinner (if hosted by bride and groom)				
Site rental				
Equipment rental				
Invitations				
Food				
Beverages				
Decorations				
Flowers				
Party favors				
Weekend wedding parties				

Item	Projected Cost (including tax, if applicable)	Deposit Paid	Balance Due	Who Pays?
CEREMONY				
Location fee				
Officiant's fee				
Donation to church (optional, amount varies)				
Organist				
Tip (amount varies)				
Other musicians				
Tip (amount varies)				
Program				
Aisle runner				
BUSINESS AND LEGAL MATTERS				
Marriage license				
Blood test (if applicable)				
WEDDING JEWELRY				
Engagement ring				
Bride's wedding band				
Groom's wedding band				
BRIDE'S FORMAL WEAR				
Wedding gown				
Alterations				
Undergarments (slip, bustier, hosiery, etc.)				
Headpiece				
Shoes				
Jewelry (excluding engagement and wedding rings)				

Item	Projected Cost (including tax, if applicable)	Deposit Paid	Balance Due	Who Pays?
Purse (optional)				
Cosmetics, or makeup stylist				
Hair stylist				
Going-away outfit				
Going-away accessories				
Honeymoon clothes				
GROOM'S FORMAL WEAR				
Tuxedo				
Shoes				
Going-away outfit				
Honeymoon clothes				
GIFTS				
Bride's Attendants				
Groom's Attendants				
Bride (optional)				
Groom (optional)				
RECEPTION				
Site rental				
Equipment rental (chairs, tent, etc.)				
Decorations				
Servers, bartenders				
Wine service for cocktail hour				
Hors d'oeuvres				
Entrees				
Meals for hired help				

Item	Projected Cost (including tax, if applicable)	Deposit Paid	Balance Due	Who Pays?
Non-alcoholic beverages				
Wine				
Champagne				
Liquor				
Dessert				
Toasting glasses				
Guest book and pen				
Place cards				
Printed napkins				
Party favors (matches, chocolates, etc.)				
Box or pouch for envelope gifts				
Tip for caterer or banquet manager (usually 15–20%)				
Tip for servers, bartenders (usually 15–20% total)				
PHOTOGRAPHY AND VIDEOGRAPHY				
Engagement portrait				
Wedding portrait				
Wedding proofs				
Photographer's fee				
Wedding prints				
Album				
Mothers' albums				
Extra prints				
Videographer's fee				
Videotape				

Item	Projected Cost (including tax, if applicable)	Deposit Paid	Balance Due	Who Pays?
RECEPTION MUSIC				
Musicians for cocktail hour				
Tip (optional, up to 15%)				
Live Band				
Tip (optional, usually $25 per band member)				
Disc jockey				
Tip (optional, usually 15–20%)				
FLOWERS AND DECORATIONS				
Flowers for wedding site				
Decorations for wedding site				
Bride's bouquet				
Bridesmaids' flowers				
Boutonnieres				
Corsages				
Flowers for reception site				
Potted plants				
Table centerpieces				
Head table				
Cake table				
Decorations for reception				
WEDDING INVITATIONS AND STATIONERY				
Invitations				
Announcements				
Thank-you notes				
Calligrapher				
Postage (for invitations and reponse cards)				

Item	Projected Cost (including tax, if applicable)	Deposit Paid	Balance Due	Who Pays?
WEDDING CAKE				
Wedding cake				
Groom's cake				
Cake top and decorations				
Flowers for cake				
Cake serving set				
Cake boxes				
WEDDING TRANSPORTATION				
Limousines or rented cars				
Parking				
Tip for drivers (usually 15–20%)				
GUEST ACCOMMODATIONS				
GUEST TRANSPORTATION				
HONEYMOON				
Transportation				
Accommodations				
Meals				
Spending Money				
ADDITIONAL EXPENSES (LIST BELOW)				
TOTAL OF ALL EXPENSES				

CHAPTER THREE

YOUR WEDDING STYLE

It's important to decide on the type of wedding you want before you can set a date, make a budget, and . . . well, before you can plan much of anything at all. Though you may be eager to view banquet halls and try on wedding gowns, figuring out your wedding style first will be time well spent, and will help you formulate answers for the many choices you'll have to make later.

Religious or Civil?

Squaring away the details of your wedding ceremony should be one of your first priorities. If you don't know the location, date, and time of your ceremony, then you certainly can't do much reception planning. You'll first need to decide whether you prefer a religious or civil ceremony. If you are interested in having a religious ceremony, consult with your officiant as soon as possible about the availability of the church or synagogue for the date you've selected, as well as to learn what restrictions and guidelines will apply (see Chapter 8 for more information about this).

An alternative for those who are unsure of their religious convictions but want to incorporate spirituality into their wedding ceremony is the nondenominational wedding ceremony. This is a spiritual ceremony without the structure and restrictions of one specific religion, although the service typically resembles a traditional Protestant ceremony. It is offered by the Unitarian Universalist church and other nondenominational groups that perform interfaith marriages for non-members.

Civil Ceremonies

Some couples of differing faiths choose to bypass the tension and potential family problems of an interfaith ceremony by having a civil ceremony. Civil ceremonies may also be the best option for couples who are unsure about their own religious convictions—or who simply prefer a small, simple, and inexpensive ceremony. The officiant in a civil ceremony is a judge or other civic official legally qualified to perform a marriage.

Contrary to the stereotype (an empty ritual in a judge's chambers that takes all of twenty seconds) "civil" does not necessarily mean boring, quick, or small. If you like, you can have a civil ceremony with all the trimmings of a traditional church wedding. Granted, it won't be in a religious setting, and no religious officials will be present, but you can still summon up a scene of power and drama. After all, your civic official isn't tied to a chair in city hall. Get him or her out of the office—and out to a hotel ballroom, a country club, a yacht, or anywhere else you feel like having your wedding. Civil ceremonies not held at city hall or the courthouse are usually held at the reception site, which tends to make things more convenient for all involved.

If you prefer to hold your ceremony in the civic official's office, think twice about your wedding attire. You may not feel comfortable coming and going in a full-length white gown. The typical dress code for this circumstance is a street-length dress or suit for the bride, and a suit for the groom.

Any further questions you have about a civil ceremony, such as who exactly will be performing it, can be resolved with a call to city hall—or whatever office in your area handles marriage licenses.

Levels of Formality

The time and location of the wedding ceremony, the type of the reception, and the attire of the wedding party and guests are just a few elements that contribute to the level of your wedding's formality. Following are some general guidelines to follow. Just remember, whatever level of formality you choose, try to keep it more or less consistent throughout.

Very Formal

- Typically held in a church, synagogue, or luxury hotel
- Two hundred or more guests
- Engraved invitations with traditional typeface and wording
- Bride and groom each have between four and twelve attendants

- Bride wears a gown with a cathedral-length train and veil, and gloves
- Bridesmaids wear floor-length dresses or gowns
- Groom and male attendants and guests wear formal attire (white tie and coattails for evening)
- Elaborate sit-down dinner, usually held in a ballroom
- Orchestra or live band
- Cascade bouquets and elaborate floral displays
- Limousines or antique cars

FORMAL

- Typically held in a church, synagogue, or luxury hotel
- One hundred or more guests
- Engraved or printed invitations with traditional wording
- Bride and groom each have between three and six attendants
- Bride wears a gown with a chapel-length or sweeping train and veil
- Bridesmaids wear floor-length dresses or gowns
- Groom and male attendants wear formal attire (black tie for evening)
- Sit-down dinner or buffet, usually held in a ballroom, banquet facility, or private club
- Live band or disc jockey
- Medium-size bouquets and floral displays
- Limousines, antique cars, or horse-drawn carriages

SEMI-FORMAL

- Held in a church, synagogue, private home, outdoors, or other location
- Fewer than one hundred guests
- Printed invitations with traditional or personalized wording
- Bride and groom each have between one and three attendants

- Bride wears a floor- or cocktail-length gown with a fingertip veil or hat
- Bridesmaids wear floor- or cocktail-length dresses
- Groom and male attendants wear suits and ties
- Reception including a simple meal or light refreshments usually held at ceremony location
- Live band or disc jockey
- Small bouquet for the bride, simple flower arrangements for decorations

INFORMAL

- Daytime ceremony often held at home or in a judge's chambers
- Fewer than fifty guests
- Printed or hand-written invitations with personalized wording
- Bride and groom each have one attendant
- Bride wears a suit or cocktail-length dress, with no veil or train
- Maid of honor wears a street-length dress
- Groom and best man wear suits and ties
- Reception including a simple meal or light refreshments usually held at home or restaurant
- Corsage or small bouquet for the bride, simple flower arrangements for decorations

Ceremony Locations

Though most couples today still wed in a church or synagogue, there are many different settings to choose from, even if you desire a religious ceremony. If you want to have a religious ceremony at a site other than your church or synagogue, be sure to consult with your officiant before making any concrete plans. Also, you should keep in mind that the location of your wedding ceremony should be in keeping with the level of formality you've chosen. For example, a church, synagogue, or mansion would be more appropriate locations for a very formal ceremony than a meadow or theme park.

Here are just a few ceremony location ideas:

- Aquarium
- Beach
- Boat, sailboat, or yacht
- Chapel
- Church/synagogue
- College or university chapel, hall, or courtyard
- Concert hall
- Country inn
- Cruise ship
- Farmhouse
- Formal garden
- Greenhouse
- Historic mansion or castle
- Hotel ballroom or banquet facility
- Lighthouse
- Meadow
- Military club
- Mountain or cliff
- Museum or art gallery
- Observatory
- Orchard
- Pier or waterfront restaurant
- Plantation
- Private club
- Private home or estate
- Public gardens or park
- Public or historic site
- Ranch
- Scenic mountain resort
- Ship, boat, or yacht
- Theater
- Theme park (Disney World, etc.)
- Vacation getaway spot (tropical island, European city, etc.)
- Winery or vineyard
- Your home or garden

Theme Weddings

A theme wedding is another step away from the traditional that can really make your wedding something special. Depending on the theme you choose, you can live out your fantasies of living in another time or another place—or in a whole new way. Here are some ideas. (Be sure to share whatever theme idea you have with your guests so they can dress appropriately.)

A PERIOD WEDDING

This theme emphasizes the traditions, costumes, music, and customs of an earlier period. Though the 1920s–1960s are the most popular periods, you could opt for Colonial America or Victorian England if you prefer . . . as long as you can find the costumes.

An Ethnic Wedding

Perhaps you and your fiancé would like to highlight the culture and costumes of your ethnic backgrounds.

A Western-Style Wedding

Cowboy hats abound here, as do fiddles, square dancing, horses, barbecue fare, and anything else about the wild frontier you want to incorporate.

A Holiday Wedding

A wedding during a holiday season can take advantage of the decorations and spirit of that time. Valentine's Day, with its emphasis on love and romance, is a popular wedding time; Christmas is favored as well. Easter and Passover are less popular because of religious restrictions, but a patriotic motif complete with fireworks might be a good idea for the Fourth of July. If you really want to go out on a limb, how about a Halloween wedding, with both the wedding party and guests coming in costume, and pumpkins for centerpieces?

A Military Wedding

Military weddings are very formal affairs and can look quite impressive, what with all of those uniformed guests and wedding party members. This type of wedding features what is perhaps the most visually stunning conclusion of them all: the newly married couple walks arm in arm from the altar beneath an archway of crossed swords! With the exception of the attire, some matters of protocol, and the use of weaponry, a military wedding can be as much like a traditional wedding as you wish.

A Double Wedding

There are several advantages to a double wedding—a single wedding ceremony during which two couples marry. You will have very special memories to share for the rest of your lives and you can save a lot of money. Before you consent to a double wedding, though, you should realistically consider your relationship with the other couple. Do you share the same vision of what your wedding day will be like, including the season and time of day, the level of style and formality, the amount of religion incorporated into the ceremony, and so on? Are you all willing to compromise on differences that may arise? If you're unsure about any of this, you may want to "just say no" rather than risk the embarrassment of two brides brawling at the wedding. In other words, you should only agree to a double wedding if the memories you and your potential fellow-bride will share for years to come are likely to be pleasant ones.

Etiquette suggests that in a double wedding, the older of the two brides proceeds down the aisle first with her wedding party, and does other key things first. As you might imagine, two full wedding parties can get rather large, so find a place that can accommodate everyone. Aside from the fact that everything is done twice, though, the double wedding can be just like any other wedding.

AN ALL-NIGHT WEDDING

This is a wedding celebration that's planned to last through the entire night. In some cases, the group rents an additional hall after the first reception. In others, the festivities continue at a private home. The wedding usually comes to a close with breakfast the next morning. Coffee, anyone?

A WEEKEND WEDDING

You've heard of an all-nighter? Well, this is an all-weekender. Usually, a weekend wedding is set up like a mini-vacation for you and your guests, and takes place at a resort or hotel. This can be a pricey option, since the wedding sponsor(s) also pays for the guests' accommodations.

A HONEYMOON WEDDING

This is not everyone's cup of tea, but, then again, not as bad as it sounds. The honeymoon wedding is akin to a weekend wedding. The guests are invited to a romantic "honeymoon"-type locale

such as a tropical resort or inn, where they can stay with the new couple for a few days. These typically are very small weddings, and the guests usually pay for their own accommodations. After the honeymoon wedding is over, the bride and groom can depart for the real (and much more private) thing.

A PROGRESSIVE WEDDING

Like to travel? In this variation, the bride and groom attend a number of wedding festivities carried on over a period of days—and located in different places! Depending upon your budget, your love of travel, and the availability of friends and relatives to celebrate, you might start with your ceremony on the eastern seaboard, have a reception in the Midwest, and wrap things up in California. (Not all progressive wedding celebrations are that far-flung; many stay in the same state, and even the same city.)

A SURPRISE WEDDING

The wedding is a surprise not to you (you hope), but to your guests. Invite people to a standard-issue party, and if those in the know can keep a secret, your guests will be completely surprised when they arrive at a wedding.

A MEMORY LANE WEDDING

Stroll down Memory Lane with your groom, family, and friends by having the wedding at a place of special significance to you as a couple. Perhaps you want to return to the college where you two met, or the park where he proposed.

A NO-FRILLS WEDDING

After all these grand suggestions, it's easy to forget that sometimes the most beautiful and enjoyable weddings are the simplest ones. Without any frills and thrills, the meaning of the marriage celebration becomes clearer, and you realize that no matter where you are, who you're with is all that's important.

Type of Ceremony: ❑ Religious ❑ Spiritual ❑ Civil

Level of Formality: ❑ Very Formal ❑ Formal ❑ Semi-formal ❑ Informal

Desired Qualities (circle all that apply):

Artistic	Festive	Quaint
Avant-garde	Fun	Relaxed
Casual	Glamorous	Romantic
Chic	Grand	Sentimental
Community-oriented	Indoor	Simple
Contemporary	Intimate	Small
Country	Large	Sophisticated
Creative	Lavish	Spiritual
Dramatic	Lively	Spontaneous
Elaborate	Luxurious	Stylish
Elegant	Outdoor	Theatrical
Ethnic	Personal	Traditional
Exotic	Picturesque	Unique
Family-oriented	Polished	Urban
Fantasy	Private	Warm

Ceremony Location:

First choice:

Second choice:

Third choice:

Personalized Elements of Ceremony:

❑ Readings ❑ Music ❑ Vows ❑ Symbolic Ceremonies:

Season/Month:

First choice: _____

Second choice: _____

Third choice: _____

Time of Day:

❏ Morning   ❏ Afternoon   ❏ Evening   ❏ Other: _____

Bride's Attire: _____

Groom's Attire: _____

Number of Desired Attendants: _____

Attendants' Attire: _____

Number of Desired Guests: _____

Wedding Theme (if any):

First choice: _____

Second choice: _____

Third choice: _____

Type of Reception:

❏ Cocktail   ❏ Champagne Brunch ❏ Luncheon   ❏ Tea

❏ Buffet Dinner ❏ Weekend Wedding ❏ Sit-Down Dinner ❏ Other: _____

Reception Location:

First choice: _____

Second choice: _____

Third choice: _____

Entertainment: _____

Other: _____

Honeymoon Ideas: _____

Notes: _____

CHAPTER FOUR

THE PEOPLE
IN YOUR
WEDDING PARTY

Having the right group of people in your wedding party can provide much comfort and laughter during this wonderful but occasionally trying time. Surround yourself with close friends and family members you can depend on and you may just find that those prewedding parties, fittings, and rehearsals go more smoothly than you expected. They may even be fun!

With good planning and a little luck, you won't have to worry about the best man losing the rings, or a bridesmaid having a tantrum because she doesn't like the color of her dress. You need your attendants to help you out of such minor disasters, not into them! By choosing the right people in the first place, you can be sure that *you* get the moral support on the big day, not someone else.

Choosing Your Attendants

Your wedding party can be as big or small as you like. Formal weddings usually have a larger number of attendants than informal ones, but you can feel free to bend tradition here if you think it's appropriate. Think about which close friends and family members you and your groom would really like to have in the wedding.

Try to select attendants who are comfortable working with people, who don't get flustered easily, and who have known you or your groom for a while. This is no time for surprises.

If you're lucky, the number of ushers will equal the number of bridesmaids; if not, you may have to do a little cutting and juggling. The general guideline is one usher for every fifty guests. One concern is that all the bridesmaids have a partner to walk them down the aisle, and to dance with them during scheduled dances at the reception. But having a couple of extra ushers is no crime: they can walk down the aisle with each other, and they probably won't shed a tear over not dancing.

As soon as you figure out who you want in your wedding party, get out there and ask them. Sometimes, because of monetary problems or other conflicts, one of your first choices may have to decline. You want to make sure you have enough time to find a replacement. Even if you're absolutely sure everyone you want will say yes, don't wait until the last minute to ask him or her. Being part of a wedding is a big and often expensive responsibility; you want to give everyone ample time to plan and save. Six months is the minimum amount of notice you should give to everyone in your wedding party.

Attendants' Duties

Unsure about what the attendants are supposed to be doing before and during the wedding? Here is a list of the traditional responsibilities.

MAID/MATRON OF HONOR

- Helps the bride with addressing envelopes, recording wedding gifts, shopping, and other important prewedding tasks
- Arranges a bridal shower (with bridesmaids)
- Helps the bride dress for the ceremony (with bridesmaids)
- Pays for her own wedding attire
- Helps the bride arrange her train and veil at the altar
- Holds the groom's ring until the appropriate point in the ceremony
- Holds the bride's bouquet while she exchanges rings with the groom
- Signs the wedding certificate (with the best man) as a witness of the wedding
- Stands in the receiving line (optional)
- Assists the bride in any additional planning

BRIDESMAIDS

- Pay for their own wedding attire
- Help organize and run the bridal shower
- Keep a gift record at the shower (usually one bridesmaid only)
- Assist the maid of honor and the bride with prewedding shopping or other tasks
- Stand in the receiving line (optional)

BEST MAN

- Organizes the bachelor party/dinner (which is optional)
- Rents (or purchases) his own formal wear
- Drives groom to the ceremony
- Holds the bride's ring until the appropriate point in the ceremony
- Gives payment check to the officiant either just before or just after the ceremony (the money is customarily provided by the groom and his family)
- Gives payment check to other service providers, such as chauffeurs and reception coordinators (if the families wish him to)
- Returns the groom's attire (if rented)

USHERS

- Rent (or purchase) their own formal wear
- Arrive at the wedding location early to assist with set-up
- See to important finishing touches, such as lighting candles (if this is required), tying bows on reserved rows of seating, and other tasks as required
- Escort guests to their seats
- Meet, welcome, and seat guests of honor (such as grandparents)
- Roll out aisle runner immediately before processional
- Straighten up and clean after ceremony
- Oversee transfer of all gifts to a secure location after reception
- Help decorate the newlyweds' car

Child Attendants

If there are any special children or young adults in your lives, you may want to ask them to be part of the wedding. Girls under the age of eight are usually flower girls or pages, or "trainbearers"; young boys are ring bearers or pages. (Girls older than eight should be junior bridesmaids, meaning they have much less responsibility than the other bridesmaids, and may wear a different dress.)

Make sure that any children you have in your wedding are mature enough not to be overwhelmed by the whole experience. Kids under four may get tired or cranky, or even worse, throw a temper tantrum. On the other hand, if you're confident they'll be able to handle things, don't shy away from including children in the wedding; they can add a wonderful innocence and charm to the proceedings.

FLOWER GIRL

The flower girl is the last person down the aisle before the bride. Traditionally, she sprinkles fresh flower petals for the bride to walk on, but many brides have been known to slip on the petals, so you may want to think twice about this. As an alternative, you could have her toss paper petals, or just carry a pretty basket of fresh flowers.

RING BEARER

The ring bearer precedes the flower girl in the procession. He carries the rings, which are displayed on a satin pillow and tied with a ribbon. For those of you who are worried about the ring bearer losing or eating your rings, don't worry; the rings he carries are fake (and to be doubly safe, perhaps sewn or otherwise secured to the pillow). The best man and maid of honor have the real ones.

PAGE OR TRAINBEARER

The only duty of the page/trainbearer is to carry the bride's train and help to arrange it neatly. Strictly speaking, this job is only necessary if the bride has a very long train. Although most people assume that pages are always boys, there's nothing wrong with girl pages.

The Bride's Parents

THE FATHER OF THE BRIDE

On the surface, the father's duty is to accompany his daughter down the aisle and "give her away." In reality, his more important (and unspoken) responsibilities are usually a) to be depressed that his daughter has grown up and no longer considers him the most important man in her life, and b) to wonder how he's going to pay for all this.

THE MOTHER OF THE BRIDE

Though you may not realize it, the mother of the bride is considered part of the wedding party. After all, your father gets his moment in the sun—why not the woman who gave you life? At the beginning of the ceremony, the mother is the last person seated before the processional begins. But, like your attendants, she has plenty to do before the wedding, including:

- Helping the bride in choosing her gown and accessories, and in assembling a trousseau
- Helping the bride select bridesmaids' attire
- Coordinating her own attire with the mother of the groom
- Working with the bride and the groom's family to assemble a guest list and seating plan
- Helping address and mail invitations
- Helping the attendants coordinate the bridal shower
- Assisting the bride in any of the hundreds of things she may need help with before the ceremony
- Occupying a place of honor at the ceremony
- Standing at the beginning of the receiving line
- In most instances, acting as hostess of the reception
- Occupying a seat of honor at the parents' table

The Groom's Parents

The groom's parents have the easiest job of all. Aside from organizing and paying for the rehearsal dinner, they simply sit at the parents' table during the reception, have their picture taken, and think about how lucky they are because they don't have to pay for all this.

Finding a Place for Everyone

If there are any special family members or friends that you couldn't fit into the wedding party but would still like to be part of the ceremony, don't despair; there are ways to fit them in. You might have them do a scripture reading, light candles, or hand out ceremony programs. Is a close friend musically talented? Perhaps he or she could sing a song or play an instrument. Be creative! Between you, your groom, and the officiant, you should have no trouble finding ways to include everyone you wish.

Gift Ideas for the Wedding Party

It's customary to show your gratitude to the wedding party by giving each member a little gift. Let them know you appreciate all the time, money, and aggravation they've spent helping to make your wedding day something you'll all enjoy.

Possible bridesmaids' gifts include:

- Jewelry (possibly something they can wear for the wedding, such as earrings or a bracelet)
- Datebook
- Stationery
- Perfume
- Beauty product gift pack
- Jewelry box
- Monogrammed purse mirrors
- Gift certificate (to a bed and bath shop, for instance)
- Something related to a favorite hobby of the bridesmaid

Possible groomsmen's gifts include:

- Monogrammed money clip or key chain
- Datebook
- Pen set
- Cologne
- Silk tie
- Travel or shaving kit
- Gift certificate (to a sporting goods store, for instance)
- Something related to a favorite hobby of the groomsman

Maid/Matron of Honor:

Name:

Address:

Telephone:

Special duties:

Bridesmaids:

Name:

Address:

Telephone:

Special duties:

Name:

Address:

Telephone:

Special duties:

Name:

Address:

Telephone:

Special duties:

Flower Girl:

Name:

Address:

Telephone:

Special duties:

Other Honor Attendants:

Name:

Address:

Telephone:

Special duties:

Name:

Address:

Telephone:

Special duties:

Name:

Address:

Telephone:

Special duties:

Best Man:

Name:

Address:

Telephone:

Special duties:

Ushers:

Name:

Address:

Telephone:

Special duties:

Name:

Address:

Telephone:

Special duties:

Name:

Address:

Telephone:

Special duties:

Ring Bearer:

Name:

Address:

Telephone:

Special duties:

Other Honor Attendants:

Name:

Address:

Telephone:

Special duties:

Name:

Address:

Telephone:

Special duties:

Name:

Address:

Telephone:

Special duties:

CHAPTER FIVE
THE GUEST LIST

Hammering out your guest list can be a smooth, effortlessly enjoyable experience—that is, if you have a tension-free family life, an endless supply of wedding funds, unlimited reception space, and a magician who'll whip up a seating plan that pleases everyone. If you're not one of the lucky .0001 percent of the population who fit into this category, you may find this process challenging.

Estimating the Guest List

You may find it helpful to let the size of your wedding determine your guest list, not vice versa. That's because a guest list has a life of its own, and will grow to enormous proportions if left unchecked. Unfortunately, if you're like most brides, the same can't be said for your budget. So before anyone even utters the words "guest list," you and your fiancé should determine what size and style wedding you want (see Chapter 3 for more information on this).

You'll also need to determine a budget with your families, which is no mean feat (see Chapter 2 for more advice on this issue). Then taking your budget into consideration, you should be able to make a rough estimate of how many guests you'll be able to accommodate. This way, you can tell your parents and future in-laws up front how many guests they are allocated, rather than finding out too late that you'll need an airplane hangar to accommodate everyone!

Setting Limits

If you end up having too many guests no matter what you try, you'll need to cut some people from the guest list. When deciding who stays and who goes, you'll need to establish rules for your guest list that you, your fiancé, and your respective families agree on, such as a "no coworkers" policy. Remember, apply all rules across the board. Making exceptions is a good way to offend others and create more headaches for yourself. Following are some policies to consider.

No Children

That you're not inviting children is usually implied to parents by the fact that their children's names do not appear on the invitation. Just to be safe, however, make sure your mother (and anyone else who might be questioned) is aware of your policy. What age you choose as a cut-off point between children and young adults is up to you, although eighteen and sixteen are common cutoffs.

No Coworkers

If you were counting on using your wedding to help strengthen business ties, this may not be the best option. But if you do need to cut somewhere, this may be the way to go.

No Thirds, Fourths, or Twice-Removeds

If you have a large immediate family and many friends, you may want to exclude distant relatives from the guest list. Again, be consistent. As long as your second cousins don't hear that your third cousins have been invited, they should understand your need to cut costs.

No Dates for Single Guests

Though you should always invite significant others of married guests, engaged guests, couples who live together, and people who are generally considered couples, it is not necessary to invite dates for unattached guests. It's a nice gesture, especially when most of the single guests won't know many other people at the wedding, as it will help them feel more comfortable. But if your budget doesn't allow it, your single guests should certainly understand. To make them feel more comfortable, it's nice to try to seat them at the same table, especially if they're around the same age. Whatever policy you adopt, however, be sure to apply it across the board.

Handling Divorced Parents

If a divorce between your parents or your groom's parents was amicable, be thankful. You won't have to plan around family tensions. If, however, the relationship between the ex-spouses is best compared to the Civil War, you'd better map out a battle plan of your own to deal with it.

Do as much as you can before the wedding to prevent any "scenes." This is your big day; you don't want anything to happen that will upset or embarrass you. Speak with the parents openly and honestly; request their cooperation and their best behavior.

To be safe, don't schedule any events that require divorced parents to interact. Seat them at separate tables, each with his or her own family and friends. If necessary, have their tables situated as far away from each other as you can. Try to avoid offending anyone—your mother may be upset if her table is by the door while your father's is next to the head table. Also be sure to apprise the appropriate wedding professionals of any such situations. For example, you don't want your wedding photographer to unwittingly pose your divorced parents together in photos.

Out-of-town Guests

Since your out-of-town guests will be traveling some distance to be with you on the big day, you should try to make things as pleasant and convenient for them as possible. Start by helping them find a place to hang their hats over the course of their stay, whether it be with family members, with friends, or in local hotels. Generally, guests pay for their own lodging (unless either the bride's or groom's families can offer to pick up the tab), but it is customary for you to make reservations for them, or at least provide enough information so that they can do it themselves.

Some hotels will offer a lower rate for a group or "block" of rooms. Grouping your out-of-town guests in one place has several advantages: the group rates will lighten the burden to their pockets, they can mingle with the other guests during the "down time" between wedding events, and they can carpool to and from the festivities.

Once you find out where your guests will be staying, you might go the extra mile and arrange to have a small gift awaiting them in their rooms (if your finances permit). A bottle of wine or a fruit basket would be a welcome sight to weary travelers. Another way to make your out-of-town guests feel welcome is to invite them to the rehearsal dinner, and to any other wedding events that are going on while they're in town. Inviting them makes them feel like the trip was worth it.

Don't forget to enclose detailed maps to all the events for those unfamiliar with the area. You don't want guests to have traveled across the country for your wedding, only to miss it because they got lost a few miles from the ceremony site. As a further precaution, consider putting a trustworthy friend or relative in charge of herding the out-of-town group and transporting them from place to place. This person would also be in charge of airport pick-ups and drop-offs.

If your out-of-town guests have brought children with them who have not been invited to the wedding, talk about finding a baby sitter well in advance. (Some churches have baby sitters on hand for the ceremony.) Children can be invited to the rehearsal dinner even if they're not going to the ceremony.

Name	Address	Telephone	RSVP Received?
1.			
2.			
3.			
4.			
5.			
6.			
7.			
8.			
9.			
10.			
11.			
12.			
13.			
14.			
15.			
16.			
17.			
18.			
19.			
20.			
21.			
22.			
23.			
24.			
25.			

Name	Address	Telephone	RSVP Received?
26.			
27.			
28.			
29.			
30.			
31.			
32.			
33.			
34.			
35.			
36.			
37.			
38.			
39.			
40.			
41.			
42.			
43.			
44.			
45.			
46.			
47.			
48.			
49.			
50.			

Name	Address	Telephone	RSVP Received?
51.			
52.			
53.			
54.			
55.			
56.			
57.			
58.			
59.			
60.			
61.			
62.			
63.			
64.			
65.			
66.			
67.			
68.			
69.			
70.			
71.			
72.			
73.			
74.			
75.			

Name	Address	Telephone	RSVP Received?
76.			
77.			
78.			
79.			
80.			
81.			
82.			
83.			
84.			
85.			
86.			
87.			
88.			
89.			
90.			
91.			
92.			
93.			
94.			
95.			
96.			
97.			
98.			
99.			
100.			

Be sure to give a copy of this to your mother, maid/matron of honor, and anyone else guests may contact for information about accommodations.

Blocks of Rooms Reserved for Wedding at:

Hotel:

Address:

Directions:

Approximate distance from ceremony site: _____ Reception site:

Telephone:

Toll-free reservations number:

Fax number:

Contact:

Number of single rooms reserved in block: _____ Daily rate:

Number of double rooms reserved in block: _____ Daily rate:

Total number of rooms reserved in block:

Date(s) reserved:

Cutoff/Last day reservations accepted:

Terms of agreement:

Payment procedure:

Notes:

Hotel:

Address:

Directions:

Approximate distance from ceremony site: Reception site:

Telephone:

Toll-free reservations number:

Fax number:

Contact:

Number of single rooms reserved in block: Daily rate:

Number of double rooms reserved in block: Daily rate:

Total number of rooms reserved in block:

Date(s) reserved:

Cutoff/Last day reservations accepted:

Terms of agreement:

Payment procedure:

Notes:

Other Nearby Lodgings:

Hotel:

Address:

Directions:

Approximate distance from ceremony site: Reception site:

Telephone:

Toll-free reservations number:

Daily room rate:

Notes:

Hotel:

Address:

Directions:

Approximate distance from ceremony site: Reception site:

Telephone:

Toll-free reservations number:

Daily room rate:

Notes:

CHAPTER SIX
BRIDAL SHOWERS AND OTHER PREWEDDING PARTIES

The Bridal Shower

Once you've chosen your bridesmaids, registered for gifts, started the battle of the guest list, and convinced your father that a backyard barbecue isn't exactly the kind of reception you have in mind, your female relatives and friends will probably start whispering about wedding showers. These little gatherings, in which your friends "shower" you and your fiancé with gifts, are usually held long after the dust from your engagement party has settled, but no less than two weeks prior to the wedding.

In the past, etiquette dictated that a bridal shower could only be sponsored by your friends; today, as with many things related to weddings, that has changed. Family, friends, coworkers, and anyone else who feels so inclined may throw a shower for you. The most common sponsors are your bridal party, in combination with your mother and other close family members—but who's to say what other generous (and ambitious) people might serve as hosts.

The typical shower is held either at a small function hall or in someone's home, depending on the size of the guest list. The guests are women only, but your fiancé may come along for the ride so he can spend the time looking awkward as you open box after box, especially the ones with lingerie inside.

By the way, it was customary in the past to keep the specifics of the shower—time, date, location, and so on—a secret from the bride until the last possible moment. These days, however, it is a little more common for the bride (who may have a busy work schedule) to take an active part in planning the festivities.

INVITES AND VITTLES

Showers are generally informal. You may wish to send invitations (you can buy them ready-made in any stationery store) or, if the guest list is small enough, invite guests via telephone. It is customary to provide your guests with refreshment (remember, they will have to sit for two exhausting hours "oohing" and "ahhhing" while you open present after present). The menu can be as simple or as complicated as the hosts want it to be; there are no etiquette rules to follow here. Of course, if the guest list (and the

budget) is big enough, your hosts may wish to hire a caterer to lower the hassle factor.

Bridal Shower

For Joan Smith
Saturday, April 25th
233 Graham Lane, Dover
Three o'clock

R.S.V.P.

THE GIFT RECORDER

The most important thing to remember for any shower is to assign someone the task of keeping track of your gifts. If you have already purchased a gift recorder, great; if not, any kind of notebook will do. Put someone you trust in charge of recording what each gift is, and most importantly, who sent it. That way, you can properly write out your thank-you notes after the shower.

THEME SHOWERS

At a theme shower, guests are told to bring a gift that fits in with a set theme, such as a kitchen shower, a linen shower, a lingerie/personal shower, a recreation shower, a honeymoon shower, and so on.

Some theme showers dictate the guest list and the menu. In a Jack and Jill shower, for instance, the women bring their husbands or significant others, presumably kicking and screaming in protest, along to the shower. Another example is the barbecue shower, which is usually co-ed and is typically held in someone's backyard.

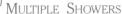

Multiple Showers

Often, different groups sponsor separate showers for the bride-to-be. Perhaps her college friends will have a small one, her coworkers another, and the groom's family yet another. In such cases, it's best if those in charge can coordinate with each other. That way, each shower can have a different theme, and there are likely to be fewer repeat gifts.

The Bachelor Party

You've heard all about this. A woman popping out of a cake, and much eating, drinking, and making merry (with emphasis on the latter two). In the past, this party was held the night before the wedding, but too many hung-over grooms and ushers have led more and more rational adults to schedule this high-culture event about a week before the wedding. Tradition dictates that the groom is to signal the end of the party with a toast to his bride.

The Bachelorette Party

Why should the guys have all the fun? These days the bride-to-be is getting her night on the town too, and the proceedings are usually a little livelier than the shower. Bachelorette parties today may consist of dinner followed by dancing, a comedy show, theatre, or concert. There are no strict guidelines to follow here except to be creative and have a blast!

The Attendants' Party

An attendants' party gives you the chance to turn the tables—to honor the people who've been honoring you. Usually this party is scheduled about a week or two before the wedding, to give all the harried planners a chance to relax and pretend to forget about the impending fuss. In a happy (for them) reversal of fortune, your guests are freed from the burden of bringing you gifts. If you and your groom wish, you may now give your attendants the gifts you've bought for them (another common time is during the rehearsal dinner). The guest list does not have to be limited to the attendants; family and close friends would probably also enjoy a breather. To keep the atmosphere relaxed, consider having a barbecue, a picnic in a park, or a day at the beach (weather permitting, of course).

The Wedding Rehearsal

If you're expecting your wedding rehearsal to go something like the final dress rehearsal for a Broadway play, you're likely to be disappointed. Sure, you'll probably have jitters that beat an opening night panic attack, but at least you won't have to worry about your officiant ordering the wedding party around like a director, screaming, "You're all going out there as rookies, but you've got to come back as stars." As anticlimactic as it sounds, the rehearsal is mainly a chance for the officiant to meet your wedding party and acquaint everyone with the basics of the ceremony.

The rehearsal is usually held the night before the wedding. (Any time during the week before the wedding is fine, though.) Everyone participating in the ceremony, including any readers or candlelighters, attend. After a brief overview of the ceremony, the officiant will talk everyone through a quick practice run-through. This time, at least, you won't have to worry about walking down the aisle "very slowly"; run, skip, and turn cartwheels if you like. Your readers should check with the officiant to make sure the version of Scripture they've been practicing in front of the mirror at home is in fact the one being used in the ceremony. (Sometimes the wording will differ from bible to bible depending on the version; only the officiant is likely to know which version will be used in the ceremony.)

The Rehearsal Dinner

By the end of the rehearsal, everyone's bound to be feeling giddy with anticipation. Time for another party! The rehearsal dinner is the last chance you'll get to relax and kick back before the big event; make the most of it. (It's possible that the idea for holding the dinner on the eve of the wedding arose because it's a convenient way to keep the bride and groom from being home alone, nervously climbing the walls.)

Traditionally, the rehearsal dinner is hosted by the groom's parents, but these days, anyone can do it. In comparison to the wedding itself, the rehearsal dinner is very relaxed. The dinner is usually held at a restaurant, a club, or a private home. There is no dress code, and no need for written invitations, unless the hosts want to send them. Otherwise, a simple phone call will suffice.

The members of the wedding party and their significant others should be invited, as well as the parents of the bride and groom. If there are any children in the wedding party, they should be present, but their parents (who should also be invited, of course) should get them home early enough to get a good night's sleep. Overtired children can be unpleasant children, and you really don't need any wedding-day temper tantrums.

If any of your out-of-town guests arrive in town in time for the dinner, you should invite them as well. This way, you'll get to spend more time with people you probably don't see that often, and they'll feel that distance hasn't kept them from being a part of the festivities. Similarly, if you have any close friends you couldn't manage to fit into the wedding party, you might want to invite them.

The rehearsal dinner is usually the time when the bride and groom hand out their gifts to the attendants, parents, and anyone else they may have bought presents for. If you follow tradition, you will make a few toasts during the party: the best man to the couple, the groom to his bride and future in-laws, and the bride to the groom and her future in-laws. But if you prefer to skip the toasts, do so, because your dinner doesn't have to include any ceremony at all. Remember, there'll be enough formality at the wedding. Feel free to just sit back, relax, and enjoy it all.

Name: _____

Address: _____

_____

Telephone: _____

❏ RSVP Number in Party: _____

Name: _____

Address: _____

_____

Telephone: _____

❏ RSVP Number in Party: _____

Name: _____

Address: _____

_____

Telephone: _____

❏ RSVP Number in Party: _____

Name: _____

Address: _____

_____

Telephone: _____

❏ RSVP Number in Party: _____

Name: _____

Address: _____

_____

Telephone: _____

❏ RSVP Number in Party: _____

Name: _____

Address: _____

_____

Telephone: _____

❏ RSVP Number in Party: _____

Name: _____

Address: _____

_____

Telephone: _____

❏ RSVP Number in Party: _____

Name: _____

Address: _____

_____

Telephone: _____

❏ RSVP Number in Party: _____

Name: _____

Address: _____

_____

Telephone: _____

❏ RSVP Number in Party: _____

Name: _____

Address: _____

_____

Telephone: _____

❏ RSVP Number in Party: _____

Name: _____

Address: _____

_____

Telephone: _____

❑ RSVP Number in Party: _____

Name: _____

Address: _____

_____

Telephone: _____

❑ RSVP Number in Party: _____

Name: _____

Address: _____

_____

Telephone: _____

❑ RSVP Number in Party: _____

Name: _____

Address: _____

_____

Telephone: _____

❑ RSVP Number in Party: _____

Name: _____

Address: _____

_____

Telephone: _____

❑ RSVP Number in Party: _____

Name: _____

Address: _____

_____

Telephone: _____

❑ RSVP Number in Party: _____

Name: _____

Address: _____

_____

Telephone: _____

❑ RSVP Number in Party: _____

Name: _____

Address: _____

_____

Telephone: _____

❑ RSVP Number in Party: _____

Name: _____

Address: _____

_____

Telephone: _____

❑ RSVP Number in Party: _____

Name: _____

Address: _____

_____

Telephone: _____

❑ RSVP Number in Party: _____

Name: _____

Address: _____

_____

Telephone: _____

❏ RSVP Number in Party: _____

Name: _____

Address: _____

_____

Telephone: _____

❏ RSVP Number in Party: _____

Name: _____

Address: _____

_____

Telephone: _____

❏ RSVP Number in Party: _____

Name: _____

Address: _____

_____

Telephone: _____

❏ RSVP Number in Party: _____

Name: _____

Address: _____

_____

Telephone: _____

❏ RSVP Number in Party: _____

Name: _____

Address: _____

_____

Telephone: _____

❏ RSVP Number in Party: _____

Name: _____

Address: _____

_____

Telephone: _____

❏ RSVP Number in Party: _____

Name: _____

Address: _____

_____

Telephone: _____

❏ RSVP Number in Party: _____

Name: _____

Address: _____

_____

Telephone: _____

❏ RSVP Number in Party: _____

Name: _____

Address: _____

_____

Telephone: _____

❏ RSVP Number in Party: _____

Name	Description of Gift	Thank-you Note Sent?

Name	Description of Gift	Thank-you Note Sent?

Name: _____

Address: _____

_____

Telephone: _____

❑ RSVP

Name: _____

Address: _____

_____

Telephone: _____

❑ RSVP

Name: _____

Address: _____

_____

Telephone: _____

❑ RSVP

Name: _____

Address: _____

_____

Telephone: _____

❑ RSVP

Name: _____

Address: _____

_____

Telephone: _____

❑ RSVP

Name: _____

Address: _____

_____

Telephone: _____

❑ RSVP

Name: _____

Address: _____

_____

Telephone: _____

❑ RSVP

Name: _____

Address: _____

_____

Telephone: _____

❑ RSVP

Name: _____

Address: _____

_____

Telephone: _____

❑ RSVP

Name: _____

Address: _____

_____

Telephone: _____

❑ RSVP

Name:

Address:

Telephone:

❏ RSVP

Name:

Address:

Telephone:

❏ RSVP

Name:

Address:

Telephone:

❏ RSVP

Name:

Address:

Telephone:

❏ RSVP

Name:

Address:

Telephone:

❏ RSVP

Name:

Address:

Telephone:

❏ RSVP

Name:

Address:

Telephone:

❏ RSVP

Name:

Address:

Telephone:

❏ RSVP

Name:

Address:

Telephone:

❏ RSVP

Name:

Address:

Telephone:

❏ RSVP

Name:

Address:

Telephone:

❑ RSVP

Name:

Address:

Telephone:

❑ RSVP

Name:

Address:

Telephone:

❑ RSVP

Name:

Address:

Telephone:

❑ RSVP

Name:

Address:

Telephone:

❑ RSVP

Name:

Address:

Telephone:

❑ RSVP

Name:

Address:

Telephone:

❑ RSVP

Name:

Address:

Telephone:

❑ RSVP

Name:

Address:

Telephone:

❑ RSVP

Name:

Address:

Telephone:

❑ RSVP

Name: _____

Address: _____

_____

Telephone: _____

❏ RSVP

Name: _____

Address: _____

_____

Telephone: _____

❏ RSVP

Name: _____

Address: _____

_____

Telephone: _____

❏ RSVP

Name: _____

Address: _____

_____

Telephone: _____

❏ RSVP

Name: _____

Address: _____

_____

Telephone: _____

❏ RSVP

Name: _____

Address: _____

_____

Telephone: _____

❏ RSVP

Name: _____

Address: _____

_____

Telephone: _____

❏ RSVP

Name: _____

Address: _____

_____

Telephone: _____

❏ RSVP

Name: _____

Address: _____

_____

Telephone: _____

❏ RSVP

Name: _____

Address: _____

_____

Telephone: _____

❏ RSVP

Name: _____

Address: _____

_____

Telephone: _____

❏ RSVP

Name: _____

Address: _____

_____

Telephone: _____

❏ RSVP

Name: _____

Address: _____

_____

Telephone: _____

❏ RSVP

Name: _____

Address: _____

_____

Telephone: _____

❏ RSVP

Name: _____

Address: _____

_____

Telephone: _____

❏ RSVP

Name: _____

Address: _____

_____

Telephone: _____

❏ RSVP

Name: _____

Address: _____

_____

Telephone: _____

❏ RSVP

Name: _____

Address: _____

_____

Telephone: _____

❏ RSVP

Name: _____

Address: _____

_____

Telephone: _____

❏ RSVP

Name: _____

Address: _____

_____

Telephone: _____

❏ RSVP

Name:

Address:

Telephone:
❏ RSVP

Name:

Address:

Telephone:
❏ RSVP

Name:

Address:

Telephone:
❏ RSVP

Name:

Address:

Telephone:
❏ RSVP

Name:

Address:

Telephone:
❏ RSVP

Name:

Address:

Telephone:
❏ RSVP

Name:

Address:

Telephone:
❏ RSVP

Name:

Address:

Telephone:
❏ RSVP

Name:

Address:

Telephone:
❏ RSVP

Name:

Address:

Telephone:
❏ RSVP

Location: _____

Telephone: _____

Contact: _____

Date: _____

Time: _____

Directions: _____

_____

_____

Number of Guests: _____

Menu: _____

_____

_____

Beverages: _____

_____

_____

Activities: _____

_____

_____

Other: _____

_____

_____

_____

Cost: _____

Notes: _____

_____

_____

_____

Wedding Rehearsal:

Location:

Telephone:

Contact:

Date:

Time:

Directions:

Notes:

Dinner:

Location:

Telephone:

Contact:

Date:

Time:

Directions:

Number of Guests:

Menu:

Beverages:

Notes:

Name: _____

Address: _____

_____

Telephone: _____

❑ RSVP Number in Party: _____

Name: _____

Address: _____

_____

Telephone: _____

❑ RSVP Number in Party: _____

Name: _____

Address: _____

_____

Telephone: _____

❑ RSVP Number in Party: _____

Name: _____

Address: _____

_____

Telephone: _____

❑ RSVP Number in Party: _____

Name: _____

Address: _____

_____

Telephone: _____

❑ RSVP Number in Party: _____

Name: _____

Address: _____

_____

Telephone: _____

❑ RSVP Number in Party: _____

Name: _____

Address: _____

_____

Telephone: _____

❑ RSVP Number in Party: _____

Name: _____

Address: _____

_____

Telephone: _____

❑ RSVP Number in Party: _____

Name: _____

Address: _____

_____

Telephone: _____

❑ RSVP Number in Party: _____

Name: _____

Address: _____

_____

Telephone: _____

❑ RSVP Number in Party: _____

Name: _____ Name: _____

Address: _____ Address: _____

_____ _____

Telephone: _____ Telephone: _____

❏ RSVP Number in Party: _____ ❏ RSVP Number in Party: _____

Name: _____ Name: _____

Address: _____ Address: _____

_____ _____

Telephone: _____ Telephone: _____

❏ RSVP Number in Party: _____ ❏ RSVP Number in Party: _____

Name: _____ Name: _____

Address: _____ Address: _____

_____ _____

Telephone: _____ Telephone: _____

❏ RSVP Number in Party: _____ ❏ RSVP Number in Party: _____

Name: _____ Name: _____

Address: _____ Address: _____

_____ _____

Telephone: _____ Telephone: _____

❏ RSVP Number in Party: _____ ❏ RSVP Number in Party: _____

Name: _____ Name: _____

Address: _____ Address: _____

_____ _____

Telephone: _____ Telephone: _____

❏ RSVP Number in Party: _____ ❏ RSVP Number in Party: _____

Name: _____   Name: _____

Address: _____   Address: _____

_____   _____

Telephone: _____   Telephone: _____

❑ RSVP Number in Party: _____   ❑ RSVP Number in Party: _____

Name: _____   Name: _____

Address: _____   Address: _____

_____   _____

Telephone: _____   Telephone: _____

❑ RSVP Number in Party: _____   ❑ RSVP Number in Party: _____

Name: _____   Name: _____

Address: _____   Address: _____

_____   _____

Telephone: _____   Telephone: _____

❑ RSVP Number in Party: _____   ❑ RSVP Number in Party: _____

Name: _____   Name: _____

Address: _____   Address: _____

_____   _____

Telephone: _____   Telephone: _____

❑ RSVP Number in Party: _____   ❑ RSVP Number in Party: _____

Name: _____   Name: _____

Address: _____   Address: _____

_____   _____

Telephone: _____   Telephone: _____

❑ RSVP Number in Party: _____   ❑ RSVP Number in Party: _____

CHAPTER SEVEN

THE GIFT REGISTRY

One of the many perks of getting married is that people shower you with gifts. The idea behind all this gift-giving is to help the new couple set up their home and start their life together. You pay these generous friends and family members back by showing them a wonderful time at your wedding—and by having a long, happy marriage.

The gifts will probably start arriving soon after you announce your engagement and continue in a steady stream until the wedding. Etiquette dictates that people have up to a year after the wedding to send a gift; so you may be getting scattered presents long after the honeymoon. A gift recorder to organize what you receive, from whom, and when is a must—one is supplied at the end of this chapter. Organizing things this way will be a great help when you sit down to write those thank-you notes.

How to Register for Gifts

Though some of your friends and family have probably already decided on the perfect gift for you, there are no doubt others who would appreciate a few hints. That's where the gift registry comes in. Gift registry is a free service provided by most department, jewelry, gift, and specialty stores. Couples "register" for a list of gifts that they would like to receive. When friends and family go into the store, they give the registry attendant your name, and he or she provides them with the list. As each item is bought, it is removed from the list, helping to prevent duplication.

You and your fiancé should put some careful thought into what store or stores you will register with. Make sure the store has a variety of quality items in the colors and styles you want. (In other words, don't pick a place because you love their bath towels but despise everything else.) You might consider registering with a few specialty shops, but have some pity on your guests—you don't want to send them traipsing all over the world. It's best to register with one high-quality department store that has almost everything you need. Another advantage of these stores is that your registry can often be sent to their branches in other cities and states—a key point for out-of-town guests.

Informing guests about where you are registered should only be done verbally. It is very bad form to include this information on a wedding or shower invitation. However, you, your attendants, and your relatives may tell guests where you are registered if they ask what you would like for a gift.

Before registering with a store, ask about the policy on returns and exchanges—you don't want to be stuck with duplicate or damaged gifts. Find out whether the store will take responsibility if you receive gifts intended for another couple, and vice versa. Though it may seem farfetched, people with names much more exotic than Smith or Jones may share their name with someone else out there; if they've both got bridal registries at the same store, there can be some mix-ups. To prevent this, the store should use your groom's name or the wedding date as an additional point of reference when asking friends and family which couple they want to buy for.

Take your time and browse through the store. Items to look for include a formal dinnerware (china) pattern, a silverware pattern, glasses, pots and pans, linens, appliances, and anything else you can think of. When you decide on the style, pattern, and color you want, add that item to the list. Try to achieve some balance in your final list; mix in everyday kitchen items with fine dishware. And even though you may feel awkward, don't be afraid to ask for a few "big-money" items like a television or a VCR; you may be helping out friends or family looking to chip in for just such a major gift.

A carefully assembled gift registry can help put you on the road to a beautiful, functioning, and well-stocked home. It will also help ensure that you don't get Art Deco when you wanted Victorian; that you aren't sitting overwhelmed in front of a pile that contains five juicers, three blenders, a neon beer sign, and a lava lamp; and that, at least at the outset of your marriage, something actually matches something else at the dinner table.

Damaged Gifts

If you receive a damaged gift, try to track down the retailer who sold the item, and ask whether it was insured. If it was, tell the person who gave you the gift so she can get her money back and perhaps buy something else. Uninsured gifts that are damaged should be quietly exchanged for the same exact item; there's no need to upset or worry the sender.

Gifts at the Reception

Gifts can get lost or damaged at the reception. Tell everyone who might be asked to pass the word that you'd prefer things be sent directly to your home. Any gifts that are brought to the reception should be put together on an out-of-the-way table or in a closet. Wait until you get home before opening anything; the chances of losing or breaking something at the reception are greater if the gifts are opened. Ask that someone be in charge of watching the gifts and making sure they find their way home.

In Case of Cancellation

If the wedding is canceled, you must return all gifts, even ones that were personalized or monogrammed. Return the gift with a small note explaining the cancellation (there's no need to give messy details). If the wedding is postponed, you can keep the gifts, but even if the wedding is delayed, do not delay your thank-you notes.

Writing Thank-you Notes

As soon as you receive a gift, you should send out a thank-you note. As hard as it will be, given the many notes you'll be writing, try to be warm and personal. Always mention the gift, and, if possible, how you and your fiancé will be using it—this small touch will prevent people from feeling that you just sent them a form letter. When sending notes for gifts you received before the wedding, sign your maiden name. Here are some examples of personalized thank-you letters.

Dear Peg and Billy,
    Thank you so much for the beautiful painting. We plan to hang it over the living room fireplace for everyone to see. The colors really brighten up the room!
    Fondly,

    Ann

Dear Aunt Mary,
    Thank you for the lovely wine glasses; they really round out our bar set. Jim and I are looking forward to your next visit, when you can have a drink with us.
    Warmest regards,

    Ann

Dear Ed,
    Thank you so much for your generous gift. Mark and I have added it to savings earmarked for our first house. Now we really feel married!
    Thanks again for thinking of us.
    Cordially,

    Ann

FORMAL DINNERWARE

Desired Quantity	Quantity Received	Manufacturer: Pattern/Model:
		Dinner plates
		Sandwich/lunch plates
		Salad/dessert plates
		Bread and butter plates
		Cups and saucers
		Rimmed soup bowls
		Soup/cereal bowls
		Fruit bowls
		Open vegetable dishes
		Covered vegetable dishes
		Gravy boat
		Sugar bowl
		Creamer
		Small platter
		Medium platter
		Large platter
		Salt and pepper shakers
		Coffeepot
		Teapot
		Butter dish
		Other:

CASUAL DINNERWARE

Desired Quantity	Quantity Received	Manufacturer: Pattern/Model:
		Dinner plates
		Sandwich/lunch plates
		Salad/dessert plates
		Bread and butter plates
		Cups and saucers
		Rimmed soup bowls
		Soup/cereal bowls
		Fruit bowls
		Open vegetable dishes
		Covered vegetable dishes
		Gravy boat
		Sugar bowl
		Creamer
		Small platter
		Medium platter
		Large platter
		Salt and pepper shakers
		Coffeepot
		Butter dish
		Mugs
		Other:

FORMAL FLATWARE

Desired Quantity	Quantity Received	Manufacturer: Pattern/Model:
		Five-piece place setting
		Four-piece place setting
		Dinner forks
		Dinner knives
		Teaspoons
		Salad forks
		Soup spoons
		Butter spreader
		Butter knives
		Cold meat fork
		Sugar spoon
		Serving spoon
		Pierced spoon
		Gravy ladle
		Pie/cake server
		Hostess set
		Serve set
		Silver chest
		Other:

CASUAL FLATWARE

Desired Quantity	Quantity Received	Manufacturer: Pattern/Model:
		Five-piece setting
		Dinner forks

CASUAL FLATWARE *(continued)*

Desired Quantity	Quantity Received	Manufacturer: Pattern/Model:
		Dinner knives
		Teaspoons
		Salad forks
		Soup spoons
		Hostess set
		Serve set
		Gravy ladle
		Cake/pie server
		Other:

CRYSTAL

Desired Quantity	Quantity Received	Manufacturer: Pattern/Model:
		Wine glasses
		Champagne flutes
		Water goblets
		Cordials
		Brandy snifters
		Decanters
		Pitchers
		Other:

CASUAL GLASS/BARWARE

Desired Quantity	Quantity Received	Manufacturer: Pattern/Model:
		Water glasses
		Juice glasses

CASUAL GLASS/BARWARE *(continued)*

Desired Quantity	Quantity Received	Manufacturer: Pattern/Model:
		Beer mugs
		Pilsners
		Highball glassses
		Decanter
		Pitcher
		Punch bowl set
		Cocktail shaker
		Ice bucket
		Champagne cooler
		Irish coffee set
		Whiskey set
		Martini set
		Wine rack
		Bar utensils
		Other:

ADDITIONAL SERVING PIECES

Desired Quantity	Quantity Received	Manufacturer: Pattern/Model:
		Sugar/creamer
		Coffee service
		Serving tray
		Relish tray
		Canapé tray
		Chip and dip server

ADDITIONAL SERVING PIECES *(continued)*

Desired Quantity	Quantity Received	Manufacturer: Pattern/Model:
		Cheese board
		Cake plate
		Large salad bowl
		Salad bowl set
		Salad tongs
		Gravy boat
		Butter dish
		Salt and pepper shakers
		Round baker
		Rectangular baker
		Demitasse set
		Other:

HOME DÈCOR

Desired Quantity	Quantity Received	Manufacturer: Pattern/Model:
		Vase
		Bud vase
		Bowl
		Candlesticks
		Picture frame
		Figurine
		Clock
		Lamp
		Framed art

HOME DÈCOR *(continued)*

Desired Quantity	Quantity Received	Manufacturer: Pattern/Model:
		Brass accessories
		Picnic basket
		Other:

SMALL APPLIANCES

Desired Quantity	Quantity Received	Manufacturer: Pattern/Model:
		Coffee maker
		Coffee grinder
		Espresso/cappuccino maker
		Food processor
		Mini processor
		Mini chopper
		Blender
		Hand mixer
		Stand mixer
		Bread baker
		Pasta machine
		Citrus juicer
		Juice extractor
		Toaster (specify two-slice or four-slice)
		Toaster oven
		Convection oven
		Microwave
		Electric fry pan

SMALL APPLIANCES *(continued)*

Desired Quantity	Quantity Received	Manufacturer: Pattern/Model:
		Electric wok
		Electric griddle
		Sandwich maker
		Waffle maker
		Hot tray
		Indoor grill
		Crock pot
		Rice cooker
		Can opener
		Food slicer
		Electric knife
		Iron
		Vacuum cleaner
		Fan
		Humidifier
		Dehumidifier
		Space heater
		Other:

CUTLERY

Desired Quantity	Quantity Received	Manufacturer: Pattern/Model:
		Carving set
		Cutlery set
		Knife set

CUTLERY *(continued)*

Desired Quantity	Quantity Received	Manufacturer: Pattern/Model:
		Knife block
		Steel sharpener
		Boning knife (specify size)
		Paring knife (specify size)
		Chef knife (specify size)
		Bread knife (specify size)
		Slicing knife (specify size)
		Carving fork
		Utility knife (specify size)
		Kitchen shears
		Cleaver
		Other:

BAKEWARE

Desired Quantity	Quantity Received	Manufacturer: Pattern/Model:
		Cake pan
		Cookie sheet
		Bread pan
		Muffin tin
		Cooling rack
		Bundt pan
		Springform cake pan
		Pie plate
		Roasting pan

BAKEWARE *(continued)*

Desired Quantity	Quantity Received	Manufacturer: Pattern/Model:
		Pizza pan
		Covered casserole
		Soufflé dish
		Rectangular baker
		Lasagna pan
		Pizza pan
		Pizza stone
		Other:

KITCHEN BASICS

Desired Quantity	Quantity Received	Manufacturer: Pattern/Model:
		Kitchen tool set
		Canister set
		Spice rack
		Cutting board
		Salad bowl set
		Salt and pepper mill
		Kitchen towels
		Pot holders
		Apron
		Mixing Bowl Set
		Measuring cup set
		Rolling pin
		Cookie jar

KITCHEN BASICS *(continued)*

Desired Quantity	Quantity Received	Manufacturer: Pattern/Model:
		Tea kettle
		Coffee mugs
		Other:

COOKWARE

Desired Quantity	Quantity Received	Manufacturer: Pattern/Model:
		Saucepan (small)
		Saucepan (medium)
		Saucepan (large)
		Sauté pan (small)
		Sauté pan (large)
		Frying pan (small)
		Frying pan (medium)
		Frying pan (large)
		Stockpot (small)
		Stockpot (large)
		Roasting pan
		Omelet pan (small)
		Omelet pan (large)
		Skillet
		Double boiler
		Steamer insert
		Wok
		Griddle
		Stirfry pan

COOKWARE *(continued)*

Desired Quantity	Quantity Received	Manufacturer: Pattern/Model:
		Microwave cookware set
		Tea kettle
		Dutch oven
		Other:

LUGGAGE

Desired Quantity	Quantity Received	Manufacturer: Pattern/Model:
		Duffel bag
		Beauty case
		Carry-on tote
		Suitcases (specify quantity and sizes)
		Garment bag
		Luggage cart
		Other:

HOME ELECTRONICS

Desired Quantity	Quantity Received	Manufacturer: Pattern/Model:
		Stereo
		CD player
		Television
		VCR
		Camcorder
		Telephone
		Answering machine
		Personal computer

HOME ELECTRONICS *(continued)*

Desired Quantity	Quantity Received	Manufacturer: Pattern/Model:
		Portable stereo
		Camera
		Other:

TABLE LINENS

Desired Quantity	Quantity Received	Manufacturer: Pattern/Model:
		Tablecloth
		Place mats
		Napkins
		Napkin rings
		Other:

BED LINENS

Desired Quantity	Quantity Received	Manufacturer: Pattern/Model:
		Flat sheets (specify full, queen, or king)
		Fitted sheets (specify full, queen, or king)
		Pillowcases (specify standard or king)
		Sets of sheets (specify full, queen, or king)
		Comforter
		Comforter set
		Dust ruffle
		Pillow shams
		Window treatment
		Down comforter
		Duvet cover
		Bedspread

BED LINENS

Desired Quantity	Quantity Received	Manufacturer: Pattern/Model:
		Quilt
		Blanket
		Electric blanket
		Cotton blanket
		Decorative pillows
		Down pillows (specify standard, queen, or king)
		Pillows (specify standard, queen, or king)
		Mattress pad
		Other:

BATH TOWELS AND ACCESSORIES

Desired Quantity	Quantity Received	Manufacturer: Pattern/Model:
		Bath towels
		Bath sheets
		Hand towels
		Washcloths
		Fingertip towels
		Shower curtain
		Bath mat
		Bath rug
		Lid cover
		Hamper
		Scale
		Wastebasket
		Other:

*Give a copy of this to your mother, maid/matron of honor,
and anyone else guests may ask about possible gift ideas.*

Name of store:

Locations:

Toll-free mail order number:

Name(s) registry listed under:

Notes:

Name of store:

Locations:

Toll-free mail order number:

Name(s) registry listed under:

Notes:

Name of store:

Locations:

Toll-free mail order number:

Name(s) registry listed under:

Notes:

Name	Description of Gift	Date Received	Thank-you Note Sent?
1.			
2.			
3.			
4.			
5.			
6.			
7.			
8.			
9.			
10.			
11.			
12.			
13.			
14.			
15.			
16.			
17.			
18.			
19.			
20.			
21.			
22.			
23.			
24.			
25.			

Name	Description of Gift	Date Received	Thank-you Note Sent?
26.			
27.			
28.			
29.			
30.			
31.			
32.			
33.			
34.			
35.			
36.			
37.			
38.			
39.			
40.			
41.			
42.			
43.			
44.			
45.			
46.			
47.			
48.			
49.			
50.			

Name	Description of Gift	Date Received	Thank-you Note Sent?
51.			
52.			
53.			
54.			
55.			
56.			
57.			
58.			
59.			
60.			
61.			
62.			
63.			
64.			
65.			
66.			
67.			
68.			
69.			
70.			
71.			
72.			
73.			
74.			
75.			

Name	Description of Gift	Date Received	Thank-you Note Sent?
76.			
77.			
78.			
79.			
80.			
81.			
82.			
83.			
84.			
85.			
86.			
87.			
88.			
89.			
90.			
91.			
92.			
93.			
94.			
95.			
96.			
97.			
98.			
99.			
100.			

THE WEDDING CEREMONY

PART TWO

THE WEDDING CEREMONY

CHAPTER EIGHT

PLANNING YOUR WEDDING CEREMONY

The wedding ceremony is often a nerve-wracking experience that takes you from being an engaged couple to being a married couple. Depending on your personal convictions, this transformation can be a religious or civil (legal) act. If you and your fiancé practice the same faith and are established members of a house of worship, this decision will be easy for you. If you practice different faiths or have been inactive in your religion, you may find this decision much more difficult. Take your time, and choose the type of ceremony you want with care (see Chapter 3 for more information on this).

If you decide on a religious ceremony, consult with your officiant about any premarriage requirements. Each religion differs in its rules and restrictions, as do different branches within the same religion. Your first meeting with the officiant should clear up most of the technical details and give you the opportunity to ask any questions you may have. After everything is settled, the way will be clear for you to personalize your ceremony with music, Scripture readings, special prayers, and even your own vows.

Meeting with the Officiant

During the meeting with your officiant, be sure to get all the details concerning rules and restrictions, your church's feeling on interfaith marriages, any required commitments to raise future children in your religion, and so on. Don't be afraid to ask any questions; you want to make sure that you and your church are on the same wavelength on these important issues.

QUESTIONS TO ASK THE OFFICIANT

Here is a list of questions you may wish to ask the officiant:

- Are the dates and times we're interested in available?
- What are the requirements for getting married in this church/synagogue?
- What are the premarital counseling requirements?
- Who will perform the ceremony? (You may be close to a particular officiant, only to find that he or she is not available at the time you want.)

❧ Are visiting clergy allowed to take part in the ceremony? If so, who will be responsible for what?

❧ What does the church or synagogue have available with regards to aisle runners, musical instruments, and musical talent? Is the church organ in good working order? What is the policy for bringing in our own organist (or other musicians)? Is there enough room at the site for additional singers and players?

❧ Are there any restrictions on decorations? On music?

❧ Will the wedding party be allowed into the ceremony site well in advance of the wedding to attend to decorations and setup?

❧ Are any other weddings scheduled for the same day? If so, is there enough time between the two ceremonies to set up decorations and otherwise get things ready?

❧ Are there any restrictions on where the photographer and videographer may stand (or move) during the ceremony?

❧ Can friends and relatives take part in the ceremony, as, say, readers or singers?

❧ Will we be allowed to hold the receiving line at the site—in the back of the church or synagogue, for instance, or in a courtyard? Is there enough room for this?

❧ What is the cost for the ceremony and the use of church or synagogue personnel and facilities? (This payment is typically referred to as a donation. It does not go to any single individual, but to the church or synagogue as a whole. These days, the suggested amount will range from $100 to $200.) The best man is traditionally responsible for giving the payment to the officiant at the ceremony's conclusion.

❧ How much parking is available?

❧ Will participation from another officiant be allowed (if yours will be an interfaith marriage)?

❧ May other cultural and religious customs be included in the ceremony?

Officiant/Clergy:

Address:

Telephone:

First Meeting:

Date and time:

Location:

Notes:

Second Meeting:

Date and time:

Location:

Notes:

Third Meeting:

Date and time:

Location:

Notes:

Fourth Meeting:

Date and time:

Location:

Notes:

Fifth Meeting:

Date and time:

Location:

Notes:

Additional Meetings:

Date and time:

Location:

Notes:

Fee:

Notes:

Date and time:

Location:

Notes:

Fee:

Notes:

Ceremony Seating

Although it's not mandatory, the bride's family usually sits on the left side of the church for a Christian ceremony, while the groom's family sits on the right. The reverse is true for Reform and Conservative Jewish weddings. If one side has many more guests than the other, you may dispense with this custom and sit everyone together to achieve a more balanced look. In Orthodox Jewish ceremonies men and women are usually segregated.

Typically parents are seated in the first row (or in the second if the attendants will be seated during the ceremony). Your siblings should sit in the second row, behind your mother and father. Grandparents sit in the third row, and close friends and relatives sit in the fourth.

In the case of divorce, the bride's natural mother has the privilege of sitting in the first row, and of selecting those who will sit with her, including her spouse, if she has remarried. Your father may sit in the second row with his spouse or significant other if your divorced parents have remained amicable; otherwise he should be seated a few rows further back.

Guests are seated as they arrive, from front to back. The mothers of the bride and groom should be seated just before the ceremony begins. Late-arriving guests are not escorted to their seats by ushers. They should take seats near the back of the church, preferably via a side aisle.

The Processional

In a Catholic processional, the bridesmaids walk down the aisle, one by one, while the ushers and best man wait at the altar. The order of bridesmaids is usually determined by height, from shortest tallest. For weddings with more than four bridesmaids, they walk in pairs. The honor attendant is next, followed by the ring bearer and flower girl. The bride then enters on her father's right arm, followed by pages (if any), who carry the bride's train. The Protestant processional is the same, except ushers may precede the bridesmaids in pairs, according to height.

Orthodox, Conservative, and Reform processions vary according to the families' preferences, devoutness, and local custom. A traditional religious Jewish processional may begin with the rabbi and cantor (with the cantor on the rabbi's right), followed by the bridesmaids walking one by one, followed by the ushers walking one by one, followed by the maid of honor, the page, and the flower girl. The bride is the last to enter, with her mother on her right and her father on her left.

The Recessional

Arm in arm, you and your new husband lead the recessional followed by your child attendants. Your maid of honor and best man are next, followed by your bridesmaids, who are paired with ushers, and your parents, followed by your groom's parents. The order of the Jewish recessional is as follows: bride and groom, bride's parents, groom's parents, child attendants, honor attendants, and bridesmaids paired with ushers. The cantor and rabbi walk at the end of the recession.

Music

Most marrying couples don't give much thought to ceremony music. With the exception of "Here Comes the Bride" (and a few other stray notes from the organ) there aren't too many pieces of music directly associated with the ceremony. But these days, more and more couples are spicing up their ceremony with a variety of songs, musicians, and singers.

Carefully selected music can provide atmosphere and enhance the mood and meaning of your ceremony. Perhaps some of the songs you pick will reflect the solemnity or the joy you feel as you and your groom begin your marriage.

If additional musicians, singers, and songs are an option you'd like to consider, consult with the officiant in charge of your ceremony. Some religions place restrictions on secular selections during the ceremony, but others may be very open to them. Ask about this well in advance.

Your best bet for finding appropriate ceremony music is to check with the musical coordinator for the ceremony site. Most religious facilities have a staff organist or choir director who can help you choose the best possible music given his or her experience. The coordinator can also recommend singers and musicians who have performed well at other ceremonies. Don't worry if you think you don't know enough about classical or "church" music; the musicians you eventually choose can offer suggestions based on the guidelines you set out.

Before you hire a full orchestra to accompany the church choir, though, remember that the cost of musicians and singers for the ceremony must fit into your overall music budget. In other words, you don't want to hire a $500 string quartet when you have only $700 allotted for ceremony and reception music. It may take some planning, but don't be intimidated; you can have wonderful music for both events with a little compromise and ingenuity.

Most ceremony music is broken up into four parts: prelude, processional, ceremony, and recessional. Each of these sections has its own function and style; you should choose music that is suitable for each.

THE PRELUDE

The prelude lasts from the time the guests start arriving until all of them are seated and the mother of the bride is ready to make her entrance. The options for music here are very broad: upbeat, slow, or a mixture of both. You want the prelude to establish a mood as well as entertain the guests while they wait.

The end of the prelude, right before the processional, is usually a good time for a soloist or choir to sing a song. During this song, the mother of the bride is seated.

THE PROCESSIONAL

This is the music that accompanies the wedding party in their jaunt down the aisle. A traditional march helps to set the pace for nervous feet—and carry the spirit of the day toward the altar.

Organist's name:

Address: _____ Telephone: _____

Fee: _____

Soloist's name:

Address: _____ Telephone: _____

Fee: _____

Name of other musician, if applicable:

Address: _____ Telephone: _____

Fee: _____

Part of Ceremony	Musical Selection	Performed By
Prelude		
Processional		
During the ceremony (list specific part below)		
Recessional		
Other		

Some processional favorites (and their composers) include:

"Waltz of the Flowers," Tchaikovsky
"Wedding March," Mendelssohn
Bridal Chorus ("Here Comes the Bride"), Wagner
"Trumpet Voluntary," Dupuis
"Trumpet Voluntary," Clarke
"Trumpet Tune," Purcell
"The Dance of the Sugar Plum Fairies," Tchaikovsky
"Ode to Joy," Beethoven
"The March," Tchaikovsky
"Ave Maria," Schubert
"The Austrian Wedding March," traditional

When it's time for you to make that long trek down the aisle, you can walk to the same piece as the bridesmaids, or to a piece chosen especially for you. Sometimes the bride will walk to the same song as the bridesmaids, but played at a different tempo.

CEREMONY MUSIC

Music played while the wedding ceremony itself takes place is called, oddly enough, ceremony music. The right music here can enhance the mood and emphasize the meaning of the marriage ceremony.

Some ceremony music favorites (and their composers) include:

"My Tribute," Crouch
"The Lord's Prayer," Malotte
"Panis Angelicus," Franck
"Now Thank We All Our God," Bach
"Saviour Like a Shepherd Lead Us," Bradbury
"Cherish the Treasure," Mohr
"We've Only Just Begun," The Carpenters
"The Unity Candle Song," Sullivan
"The Bride's Prayer," Good
"The Wedding Prayer," Dunlap

"All I Ask of You," Norbet and Callahan
"Wherever You Go," Callahan
"The Wedding Song," Paul Stookey
"The Irish Wedding Song," traditional

THE RECESSIONAL

This is your exit music. The song should be joyous and upbeat, reflecting your happiness at being joined for life to the man accompanying you back down the aisle.

Some recessional favorites (and the composers) include:

"The Russian Dance," Tchaikovsky
"Trumpet Tune," Stanley
"Toccata Symphony V," Widor
"All Creatures of Our God and King," Williams
"Trumpet Fanfare (Rondeau)," Mouret
"Pomp and Circumstance," Elgar
"Praise, My Soul, the King of Heaven," Goss

Personalizing Your Wedding Ceremony

Like many couples, you and your fiancé may be looking for something different to say and do at the altar; an alternative to the traditional wedding ceremony. If you decide to personalize your ceremony, start by considering what is important to both of you. You're in charge—so customize the proceedings to your own values and dreams. Though most religions allow some flexibility in their ceremonies these days, be sure to check with your officiant about rules and guidelines. Here are some areas that couples often personalize.

READINGS

Scripture readings at your wedding will, of course, be religious in nature, but you don't have to recycle the same ones you've heard at a dozen other weddings. Your officiant will provide you with a list of recommended readings, most of which focus on some aspect of togetherness and marriage. If you have a favorite passage you'd like to have read, ask your officiant if it would be possible to include it in the ceremony.

Vows

If you feel comfortable baring your soul before a room full of people, you may want to write your own wedding vows. If you don't feel quite that comfortable, but still find the traditional vows somewhat lacking, perhaps there is a poem or saying that expresses just how you feel. Before you break out your pad and pen to write the ultimate love sonnet or memorize the words to that special poem, let your officiant know about your intentions. Some religions can be strict about what vows must be said.

Symbolic Ceremonies

Consider including a wine ceremony or a ceremony for the lighting of the unity candle. Or, as you walk up the aisle, give a single flower from your bouquet to your mother and your groom's mother. You might also take your vows by candlelight, and have the church bells rung immediately as you are declared husband and wife. Be sure to consult with your officiant first about any restrictions. Be creative!

The Receiving Line

The receiving line receives a fair amount of bad press these days, and it's usually the first tradition to get the ax. But it doesn't have to take up an agonizing chunk of time, and can be a lot of fun for you and your guests. The receiving line enables you, your groom, and key members of the wedding party to meet and greet your guests—which is very important, since you probably will not have time to socialize with everyone at the reception. Imagine painstakingly choosing the perfect gift and traveling for hours to attend a wedding, and not even having the opportunity to congratulate the bride and groom!

Although your bridesmaids traditionally join your families in the receiving line, this often makes for a slow and tedious process. Your best bet is to keep the receiving line small. The order from the head of the line is: the bride's mother, the bride's father, the groom's mother, the groom's father, the bride, and, finally, the groom. Your honor attendant may also join you on your left, but the best man does not usually join in the receiving line.

If you're worried about the line taking up too much time, consider having a very fast, informal one at the back of the church or outside the ceremony site. You greet your guests as they file out of the building. Then everyone can hop into their cars and speed off to the reception!

If you choose to have the receiving line at the reception site, have refreshments and entertainment available for guests while they're waiting.

Location of ceremony:

Address:

Date of ceremony:

Time of ceremony:

Officiant's name:

Location fee:

Officiant's fee:

Recommended church donation:

Wedding program available?

Fee:

Part of Ceremony	Description	Notes
Processional		
Opening words		
Giving away or blessing		
Reading		
Prayers		
Marriage vows		
Exchange of rings		
Pronouncement of marriage		
Lighting of unity candle		
Benediction		
Closing words		
Recessional		
Other		

(in order, beginning at the head of the line)

Bride's mother:

Bride's father:

Groom's mother:

Groom's father:

Bride:

Groom:

Maid of honor (optional):

Best man (optional):

Bridesmaid (optional):

Usher (optional):

Bridesmaid (optional):

Usher (optional):

Bridesmaid (optional):

Usher (optional):

Bridesmaid (optional):

Usher (optional):

Bridesmaid (optional):

Usher (optional):

Other honor attendant (optional):

Other honor attendant (optional):

Notes:

CHAPTER NINE

MAKING IT OFFICIAL

The Marriage License

The criteria required to get a marriage license varies from state to state. Contact your local marriage bureau (usually at the city clerk's office) to find out what requirements you have to meet, what steps you have to take, and how much time is involved. You should start the actual license process one month before your wedding, or earlier if you'll be sending out of state for birth certificates and other records. Some states require a waiting period between application and receipt of the license, but usually it's no more than a week.

Just as you have to be sure to apply for the license in time, you must guard against getting it too early, as marriage licenses do expire. In some states they may be good for 180 days; in others, only 20.

The blood test you may need to take as part of the license process protects you, your groom, and any future children from the consequences of any serious diseases either of you may have. Depending upon the state in which you are getting married, your blood sample may be screened for venereal diseases, genetic diseases, and AIDS.

THE RULES AND REQUIREMENTS

Regardless of where you get married, you will need to be aware of a number of guidelines common to all states:

- You and your groom must apply for the license together.
- You must both have all of the required paperwork (birth certificate, driver's license, proof of age, proof of citizenship).
- You must provide proof of divorce or annulment (in the case of a previous marriage).
- You must pay a fee. The fee usually ranges from $10 to $30.

WITNESSES FOR THE INSTITUTION

Plan on dragging your best man and maid of honor along when it comes time to sign the license. They need to be there as witnesses, to prove that you weren't harassed into the institution of marriage.

THE DOTTED LINE

When the time comes for you to sign the license, you should already have decided on what your married name will be. The license is the first legal document you will sign with your new (or old) name, so make sure it's what you want it to be.

SO, ARE YOU MARRIED YET?

Having a marriage license doesn't mean you are legally married; it just means you have the state's permission to get married. In order to be valid and truly binding, the license has to be signed by a religious or civil official. When the ceremony rolls around, you leave the license with your officiant. There is no going off into a back room during the ceremony (a la Charles and Di and other members of the aristocracy) to have a grand signing ceremony. The officiant simply signs the license after the completion of the ceremony and sends it back to the proper state office.

Announcing Your Marriage

If you and your fiancé are like most couples, you were probably not able to extend wedding invitations to everyone you'd like; business associates, distant relations, and others may have been squeezed off the list due to budget or space constraints. Wedding announcements are a convenient way to let people know of your recent nuptials. They are not sent to anyone who received a wedding invitation to your wedding, even if they were unable to attend. Also, you should note that people receiving announcements are under no obligation to buy you a gift.

Announcements should be mailed immediately after your wedding. You and your fiancé should have them ready before you leave for your honeymoon; your maid of honor or best man can mail them for you while you are away.

The traditional wording of announcements is as follows:

Mr. and Mrs. Joseph Moran
proudly announce
the marriage of their daughter
Margaret Ann
and
Mr. Justin James McCann
on Saturday, the third of July
One thousand nine hundred and
ninety three
at the Holy Trinity Lutheran Church,
Chicago, Illinois.

Naturally, whoever is named on the invitations as the wedding's sponsor should also be the person or persons announcing the marriage.

AT-HOME CARDS

You may also send at-home cards with your wedding announcements. These cards include your new address and when you'll be moved in and ready to accept visitors. At-home cards are also an easy way to let people know whether you have taken your husband's name and how you prefer to be addressed after you're married.

NEWSPAPER ANNOUNCEMENTS

After you've sent out individual announcements, you may choose to formally announce your wedding in the newspapers of your hometown, your fiancé's hometown, and the town in which you currently reside. The information is pretty standard: the names, occupations, and alma maters of the bride and groom; the names and towns of their parents; and the wedding location, honeymoon plans, and town in which the bride and groom will reside.

Some newspapers have a standard form you need to fill out; check with your local paper for specifications. If your newspaper does not have a standard form, you may use the Newspaper Wedding Announcement Worksheet that follows.

Newspaper Wedding Announcement Worksheet

To appear in _____ newspaper on _____ (date.)

Name(s) of sender: _____

Address: _____

_____

Telephone number with area code: _____

ॐ ॐ ॐ

_____ and _____

(bride's first, middle, and maiden names)   _(groom's first, middle, and last names)_

were married at _____ in _____ .

        (name of church or synagogue)   _(town)_

The bride, _____ ,

        (optional: name change information, for example, "will continue to use her surname")

is the daughter of Mr. and Mrs. _____ of _____ .

                (bride's parents' names)   _(their city, if out of town)_

She graduated from _____ and is a/an _____

        (optional: name of college or university)   _(job title)_

at _____ . The bridegroom, son of Mr. and Mrs. _____

(name of employer)   _(groom's parents' names)_

of _____ , graduated from _____ and

(their city, if out of town)   _(optional: name of college or university)_

is a/an _____ at _____ . The couple will live in

        (job title)   _(name of employer)_

_____ after a trip to _____ .

        (city or town)   _(honeymoon location)_

Changing Your Name, or Not

You've probably always taken your own surname for granted. But faced with its possible loss, you may find yourself more attached to the old girl than you'd realized. This is the name you went through school with, the name you went to work with, the name you made friends with, the name everyone knows you by. How can you let it go? On the other hand, maybe your last name is ten syllables long, or no one can ever pronounce or spell it right, and you can't wait to get rid of it.

If taking your husband's name is an easy decision, congratulations. Your life is much simpler than that of a lot of people. (For one thing, you can skip the rest of this chapter!) For many brides, however, the decision is quite difficult. In the past, it was very rare for a married woman to keep her own name. Now it's very common; there are even multiple options to accommodate just about any name combination or situation. If you are in a quandary over names, remember that these days the only ones who'll probably care are you, your husband, and perhaps your present and future family. So don't let the "What will everyone think?" problem worry you at all.

SPREADING THE NEWS

You can inform people of your decision on the name question in one fell swoop, or through a series of individual notices. A newspaper announcement will reach the most people the fastest; for a more personal touch, you can send out at-home cards (see the chapter on stationery) that include your name choice. As for the wording of these announcements, you can be very subtle: "The bride will keep her name" or, to really make sure everyone gets the message, "Jennifer Andrews and Richard Miller wish to announce that both will keep their present names for all legal and social purposes" or "Jennifer Andrews announces that she will take the surname Miller after her marriage on June 5, 1993."

Information to Be Changed	Name of Institution	Notified of Name Change?	Notified of Change of Address?	Notified of Change in Marital Status?
401k accounts				
Automotive insurance				
Bank accounts				
Billing accounts				
Car registration				
Club memberships				
Credit cards				
Dentist				
Doctors				
Driver's license				
Employment records				
Homeowner's/ Renter's insurance				
IRA accounts				
Leases				
Life insurance				
Loans				
Medical insurance				
Other insurance accounts				
Passport				
Pension plan records				
Post office				
Property titles				
Safety deposit box				
School records				
Social Security				
Stocks and bonds				
Subscriptions				
Telephone listing				
Voter registration records				
Wills/Trusts				
Other (list below)				

Information to Be Changed	Name of Institution	Notified of Name Change?	Notified of Change of Address?	Notified of Change in Marital Status?
401k accounts				
Automotive insurance				
Bank accounts				
Billing accounts				
Car registration				
Club memberships				
Credit cards				
Dentist				
Doctors				
Driver's license				
Employment records				
Homeowner's/ Renter's insurance				
IRA accounts				
Leases				
Life insurance				
Loans				
Medical insurance				
Other insurance accounts				
Passport				
Pension plan records				
Post office				
Property titles				
Safety deposit box				
School records				
Social Security				
Stocks and bonds				
Subscriptions				
Telephone listing				
Voter registration records				
Wills/Trusts				
Other (list below)				

CHAPTER TEN

STYLE FOR
THE AISLE

Imagine that you're a contestant on a new game show, "Let's Make a Wedding Deal." After you solve the puzzle correctly, Monty Hall directs your attention to the prize stage. Behind Door Number One are all the components necessary for the most formal of weddings: a date at an ornate cathedral, white tie and tails, and an elegant sit-down reception dinner with strolling violinists. Behind Door Number Two are the makings of a quaint, cozy wedding: a sunny backyard garden, bright yellow tent, and a luncheon buffet. Which door would you pick?

In the real world, of course, you have a much broader range of choices, but the way you answer that question will go a long way toward dictating the style and formality of your wedding attire. Granted, selecting the right wedding gown is difficult, but when it comes to picking attire to match the formality or informality of the occasion, brides actually have it a little easier than grooms. As long as her gown fits in with the overall style of the wedding (and looks good on her), the bride doesn't have much else to worry about.

A man's wedding attire, on the other hand, is much more subject to the degree of formality, the season, and the time of day. This may seem like cause for cheer—finally, something that's more complicated for men than women! But, alas, things aren't as bad as they seem for your groom. Once he knows the answer to the "Let's Make a Wedding Deal" question, just about any formalwear shop can point him (and his attendants) in the right direction.

Your Wedding Gown

Wedding gowns can take up to six months or more after the order is placed to arrive in your hands, so start wading through that sea of satin, silk, taffeta, chiffon, brocade, shantung, and organza as soon as you can. Leave yourself time for alterations and unforeseen glitches. Obviously, no book can tell you what style and fabric are best for you. But don't worry—your instinct will pull you through, and when you find the right dress, you'll know.

You'll want to take one person shopping with you (your mother or a close friend, for instance) to consult with on matters of style and appearance, and to fight with when you get frustrated because you don't like any of the fifty dresses you've tried on. It's wise not to take any more than one lucky person with you; the situation is stressful enough without inserting the opinions of five other people. If you try to please everyone, you'll never find anything, so stick with one person you trust.

Bridal Salons

If you're like most non-sewing brides, you'll be hitting the bridal salons in your area to find your dream gown. Most salons require an appointment; you can usually get one a day or two after you call. Making an appointment is worth your trouble, as they ensure the staff will give you the proper amount of attention. Don't be surprised if you feel like Cinderella being fitted for the magic slipper. The salon people are hoping lavish treatment from them will gain them lavish amounts of money from you. Be careful. Smiles, compliments, and free coffee and tea do not necessarily translate into quality dresses or reputable business practices.

SOME CAVEATS

Even if you have an unlimited amount of money to spend on a gown, you want to be sure you're shopping at a reputable shop—meaning one that won't leave you standing at the altar in your slip. Unfortunately, there are a large number of bridal shop operators out there who will try to get as much money out of you as they possibly can and, in exchange, provide little or no quality. Some tricks of the trade to be aware of are:

> ✺ The majority of salons will require a deposit equal to half the price of the dress. Rather than ordering the dress from the manufacturer right away, they'll hold your deposit and use the money for other things (like earning interest in the company checking account). They end up ordering your gown at the last possible minute, which means it may not be ready in time for the wedding.

🌺 For both wedding gowns and attendants' dresses, a shop may grossly overestimate the size a woman takes in order to charge a hefty fee for alterations. Petite women who normally take a size 4 may find themselves being told to order a size 12 dress.

🌺 If it sounds too good to be true, it probably is. A salon may offer a great price on a dress, only to charge a small fortune in alteration fees. These rip-off artists get their money one way or another.

How can you survive in this war zone? Arm yourself with these weapons:

🌺 Always talk to the manager or, even better, the owner. Find out how long the shop has been in business; one would hope that a disreputable establishment would not be able to survive for long. Ask if you can speak with a former customer to get her impression of the shop.

🌺 Always ask in advance about the price of alterations. Establish a flat rate, so you can't be hit with additional bills later on.

🌺 Find out exactly when the shop plans on ordering your dress. Ask for verification of the order, and call periodically to check on its progress.

🌺 Get every aspect of your gown's purchase down in writing, including the delivery date. Find out the store's policy regarding late or damaged gowns. If something should go seriously wrong, don't be afraid to take legal action.

HEIRLOOM/ANTIQUE GOWNS

With the price of most antiques these days, you wouldn't think an antique (or heirloom) gown would be a bargain, but it can be. Antique and heirloom gowns can be significantly less expensive than new ones, and the added style and nostalgia they provide is beyond price. The downfall of heirloom gowns is that unless you're fairly petite, you may have a hard time finding one that will fit you. Apparently, women were a lot smaller years ago.

Used/Consignment Gowns

Another way to get an inexpensive gown is to shop consignment stores and other bargain outlets for previously worn gowns. These gowns can be bought for as little as $100, and can be taken home with you that day. Of course, finding a quality wedding gown on consignment may require some tenacity, as well as a little detective work, since they can be scarce. If you're serious about taking the previously worn route, check the classified section of the local newspaper.

As with any gown you buy, you'll want to check for quality: there should be no stains, rips, or other flaws. The downside to previously worn gowns is finding someone to alter the gown for you. As bridal salons will not work on any gown that is not bought out of their store, you'll have to search for a reliable seamstress to do the alterations for you. Talented seamstresses that can do the work you require in time for your wedding do not grow on trees, and the expense of these alterations may nullify the money you saved buying the used gown. If at all possible, try to get a written estimate of the costs from your seamstress before you actually purchase the gown.

Bridal Accessories

You've found the perfect dress. Perhaps you're thinking, "No more anguished searching; goodbye to the bridal shop until my dress comes in." However, you still need a veil and headpiece.

Your headpiece and veil should complement the style of your dress; don't pick something so ridiculously elaborate that it overpowers you and your dress. You want all eyes focused on you, the complete package, not you, the little body and tiny head under a massive headpiece.

Today's wedding veils are benefiting from one of our most popular modern conveniences: Velcro! Thanks to Velcro, veils can now be removed from the headpiece after the ceremony, which frees the bride from worrying about ripping her veil during close encounters with family and friends. A Velcro veil may not sound very elegant, but talk to a bride that's had her head yanked because someone's hand or ring got caught in her veil, and you'll gain a new appreciation for the concept.

Although a headpiece takes only eight to ten weeks to arrive after you order it, you should try to give yourself more time than that. Having the headpiece well in advance gives you a chance to go through one or two trial runs with your hairdresser.

Although salons offer slips, nylons, bras, and shoes, these items are often overpriced and better found elsewhere. As long as your slip doesn't require a hoop or any other fancy stuff, you should be able to find a reasonably priced one at a lingerie shop. Don't forget to look at bras and nylons while you're there. If your gown is floor length, you can save a great deal on shoes by buying yourself a simple white (or whatever color best matches the dress) pair at a regular shoe store and decorating them yourself with lace and buttons. Why pay a fortune for shoes that no one will even see?

Hiring a Tailor

If the salon where you purchased your dress offers affordable and reliable alterations, great! That's one less detail you'll have to worry about before the big day. However, if you bought your dress second-hand, are wearing an heirloom gown, or you opted not to use your bridal salon's tailoring services, you'll need to hire a tailor of your own. Try to get a referral from another bride, your wedding consultant, or perhaps even a bridal salon. A tailor can make or break your gown, so to speak, so avoid simply picking one out of the telephone book.

Your tailor should have extensive experience working on wedding gowns and with delicate fabrics. Does the tailor offer pressing and steaming services? If not, you'll have to hire a dry cleaner to perform that job a few days prior to your wedding. The tailor should also be able to give a detailed description of the alterations that are necessary, and he or she should be willing to give you a written advance estimate and ready date.

Bridal Beauty

Have you ever been warned never to get your hair cut before getting your picture taken because "you'll look like a stranger in your own hair"? True, you usually do feel a little self-conscious after some serious scissor work, and you don't want that feeling translated forever onto film. If heeding that warning is prudent in everyday life, the advice quadruples in value when talking about your wedding. Never get a haircut or change your hairstyle right before your wedding. Not only do you run the risk of looking like "a stranger in your own hair," but you could absolutely HATE the new do, depressing you to the point where you can't truly enjoy the big day.

It's only natural to want to try a new hairstyle for your wedding; perhaps after wearing your hair down for 1,257 days in a row, you'd like to try it up, or vice versa. Or maybe you're looking for a style that really complements your headpiece. This is fine. As most politicians will tell you, change is a wonderful thing. Just make the changes in enough time before the wedding so that you can get acquainted with your new hair or, if necessary, attend to any disasters.

You should probably start experimenting with your hairdresser six months or so before the wedding. After you find the look you want, visit the shop periodically for maintenance. Bring your headpiece to your hairdresser to go through at least one trial run before the big day. Through all this you may get a little sick of the sight of your hairdresser, but feeling that you look the best you ever have for the biggest event of your life is miraculous medicine.

Hair Prep On Your Wedding Day

If you feel confident in your ability to style your own hair to your liking, there's no need to make a trip to the salon on your wedding day. But if you're like most women, you'll reach for the security of the stylist, either because you feel no one can make you look better or because your hands are too shaky to wield a brush. Brides walking out of a salon, hair all done up, headpiece in place, wearing a T-shirt and jeans are a humorous but not uncommon sight. If you don't want to be seen in public this way, see whether your hairdresser would be willing to make the trip to your home, or wherever you may be getting ready that day. This might also save you the trouble of exposing your perfect hairdo to wind and rain.

PUTTING YOUR FACE ON

If you've always wanted to sit down at one of those department store cosmetic counters and tell the attendant, "Go for it,
make me beautiful!" (that is, more beautiful than you already are),
there's no time like now to fulfill that urge. Like your hairdresser, a
cosmetologist can help you feel more confident in your appearance, or give you a completely new look. Even if you're happy
with your daily makeup selection and application skills, you may
want to try something different and special for your wedding day.
Consider your face a blank piece of paper, and your cosmetologist
a renowned artist. She can show you just what colors to apply,
what angles to apply them at, and other tricks to make your face
into a real work of art.

A department store cosmetologist will gladly give you a free consultation and a makeover, especially if it induces you to buy some of
her products. If you are completely impressed by her abilities and
her advice, buy whatever items you want and go home to practice
yourself. Don't be afraid to ask questions, or to go back if you find
things just don't look the same when you do them as when she did.
If you're unhappy with the treatment you get at one product's
counter, or feel you looked more like Bozo the Clown than a cover
girl after your makeover, don't despair; try another counter. There
are plenty of product lines and cosmetologists out there who are
more than willing to meet your needs—and get your business.

The alternative to a department store cosmetologist is a professional cosmetologist, whose business it is to make people over, not
sell a product. Instead of the department store, you go to his or
her place of business to be made over. (You'll do a couple of test
runs.) The real bonus is that, come your wedding day, you're not
left to your own devices; he or she will come to your home and
do it all for you.

Remember, after all the hair styling and makeup, the thing that
truly makes a bride most beautiful is the glow she wears that comes
from inside, from all the love and joy she's feeling on her wedding
day. That's the one thing you don't have to worry about buying or
creating: you already have it.

Bridal salon:

Name of salon:

Address:

Telephone:

Salesperson: Store hours:

Directions:

Notes:

Wedding Gown:

Description:

Manufacturer:

Style number: Color:

Cost: Order date:

Deposit paid: Date:

Balance due: Date:

Delivery date and time:

Delivery instructions/Pick-up date:

Notes:

Headpiece and Veil:

Description:

Manufacturer:

Style number: Color:

Cost: Order date:

Deposit paid: Date:

Balance due: Date:

Delivery date and time:

Delivery instructions/Pick-up date:

Notes:

Bridal Accessory	Description	Cost	Where Purchased (if different from above)	Picked Up?
Slip				
Bra				
Hosiery				
Garter				
Gloves				
Shoes				
Jewelry				
Other				

HAIR STYLIST

Name:

Salon:

Address:

Telephone: Hours:

Consultations:

Date: Time:

Date: Time:

Date: Time:

Wedding Day Appointment:

Location:

Date: Time: Number of hours:

Services included:

Total cost of services: Overtime cost:

MANICURIST/PEDICURIST

Name:

Salon:

Address:

Telephone: Hours:

Wedding Day Appointment:

Location:

Date: Time: Number of hours:

Services included:

Total cost of services: Overtime cost:

MAKEUP ARTIST

Name:

Salon:

Address:

Telephone:

Hours:

Consultations:

Date: Time:

Date: Time:

Date: Time:

Wedding Day Appointment:

Location:

Date: Time: Number of hours:

Services included:

Total cost of services: Overtime cost:

Travel fee (if applicable):

Notes:

The Groom's Attire

As it turns out, the men have it easy once again. Give them the following list, lead them to the proper rack, and all they have to do is pick out the right size and stand around for a few minutes getting measured for alterations (and perhaps stuck with a few stray pins). All that's left for them to do is to remember to pick the suit up. After being spoiled by such simplicity, what man wouldn't fall to pieces if he had to undertake the search for the right wedding gown?

Informal wedding:

- Business suit
- White dress shirt and tie
- Black shoes and dark socks
- (For the winter, consider dark colors; in the summer, navy, white, and lighter colors are appropriate.)

Semiformal wedding (daytime):

- Dark formal suit jacket (in summer, select a lighter shade)
- Dark trousers
- White dress shirt
- Cummerbund or vest
- Four-in-hand or bow tie
- Black shoes and dark socks

Semiformal wedding (evening):

- Formal suit or dinner jacket with matching trousers (preferably black)
- Cummerbund or vest
- Black bow tie
- White shirt
- Cufflinks and studs
- Formal wedding (daytime):

- Cutaway or stroller jacket in gray or black
- Waistcoat (usually grey)
- Striped trousers
- White high-collared (wing-collared) shirt
- Striped tie
- Cufflinks and studs

Formal wedding (evening):

- Black dinner jacket and trousers
- Black bow tie
- White tuxedo shirt
- Waistcoat
- Cummerbund
- Cufflinks

Very formal wedding (daytime):

- Cutaway coat (black or gray)
- Wing-collared shirt
- Ascot
- Striped trousers
- Cufflinks
- Gloves

Very formal wedding (evening):

- Black tailcoat
- Matching striped trousers trimmed with satin
- White bow tie
- White wing-collared shirt
- White waistcoat
- Patent leather shoes
- Studs and cufflinks
- Gloves

Tuxedo Shop:

Name:

Address:

Telephone: Salesperson:

Store hours:

Directions:

Services included:

Groom's Attire:

Tuxedo style and color:

Cost: Order date:

Deposit paid: Date:

Balance due: Date:

Fitting date #1:   Time:

Fitting date #2:   Time:

Pick-up date and time:

Return date and time:

Late fee:

Terms of cancellation:

Groom's Measurements:

Groom's height: Weight:

Coat size: Arm inseam:

Pants waist: Length (outseam):

Shirt neck: Sleeve:

Shoe size: Width:

Accessory	Size	Color	Cost	Where Purchased (if different from above)	Picked Up?
Tie/Ascot					
Cummerbund					
Pocket handkerchief					
Suspenders					
Studs					
Cufflinks					
Formal socks					
Shoes					
Top hat					
Cane					
Gloves					
Other					

Wedding Party Attire

Deciding whether the party should dress formally or casually is the easy part; the type of wedding you're planning will tell you that. Finding something everybody likes and looks great in, however, opens a whole new can of worms. (You may end up concluding it would be easier to dress the worms.)

First, you should decide on your wedding colors. These should be colors you really like, because you'll be seeing them on your bridesmaids, your flowers, your wedding favors, your decorations, and even your cake. If you have a couple of favorites that go well together, go with them. If your favorites happen to clash, you might consider picking only one.

Are you in a quandary as to what colors to pick? There are some guidelines that can help you decide. If your wedding will be in one of the warmer months, cool pastel shades like ice blue and pale pink work very well. In cooler months, forest green, midnight blue, burgundy, or other warm tones can give the wedding a cozy feel.

Start looking for your bridesmaids' dresses as soon as you finalize the wedding party. The women need to begin the process early because their dresses have to be made or altered.

THE BRIDE'S ATTENDANTS

When searching for bridesmaids' gowns, avoid outfits that look great on one or two people but lousy on everyone else. Try to find something everyone finds acceptable. It's not fair to make your bridesmaids wear a style that is wrong for them just because you like it. Even if something is unflattering on only one bridesmaid, it's wise to forget that style and find something else; you don't want anyone to feel awkward or unattractive. These are special people in your life; don't make them feel self-conscious. Remember, they are paying good money for dresses they will most likely never wear again; help them to feel beautiful and comfortable that one day.

Traditionally, the members of the bridal party wear the same style of dress, but you shouldn't be afraid of a little variety. Consider having everyone wear the same style of dress, but each in

153

a different color, creating a rainbow effect. If you really want to make your bridesmaids happy, allow each one to pick out whatever dress looks best on her (as long as it meets your basic color and style guidelines). This approach works especially well in a black and white wedding, with each woman wearing a different style black or black and white gown. Yet another option is to dress the bridesmaids uniformly, but to have the maid of honor wear a dress of a different style or a dress of a slightly different shade from the rest.

Attendants do not have to troop to the bridal shop as a group for fittings. Once the dresses have been ordered, they can go for alterations at their own convenience; just be sure to give them a deadline for getting it all done.

If one of your bridesmaids lives far away and can't make it to town for the fittings, ask your salon about alternate arrangements. If you can, send a photo of the dress you have in mind, and make sure it's something she will feel comfortable wearing. You might order her dress from your salon, using measurements she has provided for you, and then send it to her so she can have it altered by a local tailor or seamstress.

THE GROOM'S ATTENDANTS

The choices for men's attire are usually so simple that they're liable to drive any woman crazy. All the groomsmen dress the same, in a style and color that complement the groom's outfit. Most likely, the men will be wearing some form of tuxedo or suit, depending on the formality of the wedding. To brighten up a plain tuxedo, consider having the ushers wear cummerbunds and bow ties that match the bridesmaid's dresses.

The great majority of men rent their formalwear. Your best bet is to have your men go at least a month before the wedding to reserve their attire. In the busy wedding months between April and October, formalwear may be hard to come by; if your wedding falls during this time, make sure the guys look around and reserve things extra early.

Any male attendant who lives out of town should go to a reputable tuxedo shop in his area to be measured. Have him send the measurements to you so you can reserve his attire with the rest of the group's. Remember to ask your formalwear shop about exact prices, including alterations. Also inquire about their return policy and the time of return.

CHILD ATTENDANTS

A junior bridesmaid can wear the same dress as the other bridesmaids, or a different style that is appropriate to her age. In a black and white wedding she should not wear solid black, but a white dress with a black pattern or trimming is perfectly acceptable.

Flower girls wear either long or short dresses that match or complement the other dresses. If you have a hard time finding something appropriate, don't fret; a white dress trimmed with lace or fabric that matches the other dresses is a lovely option.

Ringbearers and male pages can dress exactly as the other men in the party, or they can wear dress shorts or knickers to make them stand out—and look extra adorable.

The Mothers

The mother of the bride usually has first choice when it comes to picking out a style and color for her gown. She then consults with the mother of the groom, who (you hope) picks out a dress color and style that complements, rather than copies, her future in-law's. It's best if their dresses don't clash with the color scheme or style of the wedding. If your bridal party is in elegant long gowns, it's doubtful you'd appreciate your mother showing up in a beaded flapper dress.

The Fathers

The fathers of the bride and groom should wear the same style and color as the attendants.

Place of Purchase:

Name:

Address:

Telephone:

Salesperson: Store hours:

Directions:

Notes:

Attendants' Attire:

Description of dress:

Manufacturer:

Style number: Color:

Cost per dress: Number ordered:

Total cost of dresses: Order date:

Sizes ordered:

Deposit paid: Date:

Balance due: Date:

Delivery date and time:

Delivery instructions/Pick-up date:

Description of alterations:

Alterations fee (total):

Description of accessories (hosiery, shoes, jewelry, etc.):

Cost of accessories:

Cost of dying shoes
(if applicable):   Color:

Notes:

Maid/Matron of Honor:

Name:

Dress size: Shoe size:

Other sizes:

Fitting date #1:   Time:

Fitting date #2:   Time:

Fitting date #3:   Time:

Notes:

Bridesmaids:

Name:

Dress size: Shoe size:

Other sizes:

Fitting date #1:   Time:

Fitting date #2:   Time:

Fitting date #3:   Time:

Notes:

Name:

Dress size: Shoe size:

Other sizes:

Fitting date #1:   Time:

Fitting date #2:   Time:

Fitting date #3:   Time:

Notes:

Name:

Dress size: Shoe size:

Other sizes:

Fitting date #1:   Time:

Fitting date #2:   Time:

Fitting date #3:   Time:

Notes:

Flower Girl's Attire:

Description of dress:

Manufacturer:

Style number: Color:

Cost per dress: Number ordered:

Total cost of dresses: Order date:

Sizes ordered:

Deposit paid: Date:

Balance due: Date:

Delivery date and time:

Delivery instructions/Pick-up date:

Description of alterations:

Alterations fee (total):

Description of accessories (hosiery, shoes, jewelry, etc.):

Cost of accessories:

Cost of dying shoes
(if applicable):   Color:

Notes:

Attendants' Attire:

Tuxedo style and color:

Cost per tuxedo: Number ordered:

Total cost of tuxedos: Order date:

Sizes ordered:

Deposit paid: Date:

Balance due: Date:

Ready date and time:

Return date and time:

Late fee:

Description of accessories (socks, shoes, studs, cufflinks, etc.):

Cost of accessories:

Notes:

Best Man:

Name:

Height: Weight:

Tuxedo style and color:

Coat size: Arm inseam:

Pants waist: Length (outseam):

Shirt neck: Sleeve:

Shoe size: Width:

Fitting date #1:   Time:

Fitting date #2:   Time:

Pick-up date: Time:

Date returned: Time:

Notes:

Ushers:

Name:

Height: Weight:

Tuxedo style and color:

Coat size: Arm inseam:

Pants waist: Length (outseam):

Shirt neck: Sleeve:

Shoe size: Width:

Fitting date #1:   Time:

Fitting date #2:   Time:

Pick-up date: Time:

Date returned: Time:

Notes:

Name:

Height: Weight:

Tuxedo style and color:

Coat size: Arm inseam:

Pants waist: Length (outseam):

Shirt neck: Sleeve:

Shoe size: Width:

Fitting date #1: _____ Time: _____

Fitting date #2: _____ Time: _____

Pick-up date: _____ Time: _____

Date returned: _____ Time: _____

Notes: _____

_____

Name: _____

Height: _____ Weight: _____

Tuxedo style and color: _____

Coat size: _____ Arm inseam: _____

Pants waist: _____ Length (outseam): _____

Shirt neck: _____ Sleeve: _____

Shoe size: _____ Width: _____

Fitting date #1: _____ Time: _____

Fitting date #2: _____ Time: _____

Pick-up date: _____ Time: _____

Date returned: _____ Time: _____

Notes: _____

Ringbearer:

Name: _____

Height: _____ Weight: _____

Tuxedo style and color: _____

Coat size: _____ Arm inseam: _____

Pants waist: _____ Length (outseam): _____

Shirt neck: _____ Sleeve: _____

Shoe size: _____ Width: _____

Fitting date #1: _____ Time: _____
Fitting date #2: _____ Time: _____
Pick-up date: _____ Time: _____
Date returned: _____ Time: _____
Notes: _____

_____

Fathers:
Name: _____
Height: _____ Weight: _____
Tuxedo style and color: _____
Coat size: _____ Arm inseam: _____
Pants waist: _____ Length (outseam): _____
Shirt neck: _____ Sleeve: _____
Shoe size: _____ Width: _____
Fitting date #1: _____ Time: _____
Fitting date #2: _____ Time: _____
Pick-up date: _____ Time: _____
Date returned: _____ Time: _____
Notes: _____

_____

Name: _____
Height: _____ Weight: _____
Tuxedo style and color: _____
Coat size: _____ Arm inseam: _____
Pants waist: _____ Length (outseam): _____
Shirt neck: _____ Sleeve: _____
Shoe size: _____ Width: _____

Fitting date #1: _____ Time: _____

Fitting date #2: _____ Time: _____

Pick-up date: _____ Time: _____

Date returned: _____ Time: _____

Notes: _____

_____

_____

Name of tailor: _____

Location: _____

Telephone: _____ Hours: _____

Description of alterations: _____

_____

Estimate: _____ Actual cost: _____

Is pressing/steaming included? _____ If no, cost: _____

Is delivery available? _____ Delivery charge (if any): _____

Deposit due: _____ Date: _____

Ready date and time: _____

Delivery instructions/Pick-up date: _____

_____

_____

Notes: _____

_____

_____

THE
RECEPTION

PART THREE

THE
RECEPTION

CHAPTER ELEVEN

PLANNING YOUR WEDDING RECEPTION

What makes a marriage ceremony a real wedding? Why, the reception afterwards, of course! If a wedding meant just standing before a religious or civic official and saying "I do," there would be precious little to have a nervous breakdown about.

The first thing you have to do regarding your reception is find a place to have it. Needless to say, that place has to be available on the day of the ceremony—unless you feel comfortable telling the ceremony guests to go home and come back the next week for the reception. Religious officiants will tell you to set the ceremony date first and find a reception site that matches, but many couples try to make the ceremony date conform to the date their desired reception site is open.

During peak wedding months (April–October), competition for reception sites can be heavy. If you're marrying in this time frame, you should probably plan on looking for a site at least a year in advance.

Choosing a Location

While function halls, country clubs, and hotel ballrooms are still the most popular sites for receptions, these days there's no limit to where you can go. As long as people can gather there to eat, drink, and be merry, it will do. Here's a list of potential sites to consider:

- Aquarium
- Beach
- Boat, sailboat, ship, or yacht
- Castle, estate, or historic mansion
- College or university hall or courtyard
- Concert hall
- Country inn
- Cruise ship
- Farmhouse
- Formal garden
- Greenhouse
- Historic mansion or castle
- Hotel ballroom or banquet facility
- Lighthouse
- Meadow
- Military club
- Mountain
- Museum or art gallery
- Observatory

- ❀ Orchard
- ❀ Pier or waterfront restaurant
- ❀ Plantation
- ❀ Private club
- ❀ Private home or estate
- ❀ Public gardens or park
- ❀ Public or historic site
- ❀ Ranch
- ❀ Scenic mountain resort
- ❀ Sports park or arena
- ❀ Theater
- ❀ Theme park (Disney World, etc.)
- ❀ Vacation getaway spot (tropical island, European city, etc.)
- ❀ Winery or vineyard
- ❀ Your home or garden
- ❀ Zoo

Odds are that you'll pay more to secure one of these nontraditional sites than you would for a standard venue, but weigh the cost against all that you'll get for your money. In settings like these, your surroundings will say something unique about you and your new husband. Estates and manors are stately and elegant; they offer opulence, style, and, often, the ambiance of an era gone by. Many have expansive grounds for the guests to stroll, and there may be room for a tent for outdoor festivities. The works of art hanging in museums and art galleries can certainly compete with any centerpieces a caterer would provide; add a little music and you've got a reception to remember. Or what about a reception in late fall in an apple orchard—complete with chairs, tables, and a string quartet?

Granted, some of these options will depend on the season and the weather, but if Mother Nature cooperates, sites like these can make for a beautiful and memorable wedding day. (For outdoor sites, alas, you will need to establish a backup site elsewhere—or incorporate a large tent into your plans—as a precaution against inclement weather.)

STAY RIGHT WHERE YOU ARE!

Some receptions are held on the same grounds as the ceremony—the ultimate in convenience for you and your guests. Most churches and synagogues have a ballroom or function room somewhere on the premises that can be rented without much fuss.

Home-Sweet-Home

For many couples, this is the perfect solution to the reception dilemma. If you're lucky, you, your parents, or someone you know will have a house and yard big enough to accommodate your reception. The informal, relaxed atmosphere of this kind of celebration can be a lot of fun. What better way to celebrate the most important day in your life than in the house you grew up in or the backyard you played in? Surrounded by your family and friends in this environment, you'll have a memorable reception experience that places your wedding in a unique context.

Don't assume that having a home reception means your parents have to sweat in the kitchen all day preparing and serving food. If you're expecting more than fifty guests, it's best to bring in a professional caterer for the job (unless your folks really were looking forward to hanging out in the kitchen).

Keep in mind that if you're having a home or backyard reception, you should consult with your caterer about obtaining the necessary tables, chairs, and other furniture. Believe it or not, there are stores out there that rent everything from decorative arches to grandiose champagne fountains—even portable dance floors!

Questions to Ask the Reception Site Manager

Now that you know about all of the wonderful reception options open to you, it's time to pick some places and evaluate them. The reception is the part of your wedding you will most likely spend the most amount of money on. Take the proper steps from the very start to make sure you get every penny's worth. Here are some questions you should ask:

- How many people can the facility comfortably seat? How big is the dance floor?
- Is an in-house catering service offered? If it is, and if you don't wish to use it, can you bring in your own caterer? (See the section on catering for more details.)
- Are tables, chairs, dinnerware, and linens supplied? What about decorations?

❧ Is the site an appropriate one for live music? Is there proper spacing, wiring, and equipment?

❧ Does the site coordinator have any recommendations for setup and decorations? Are there any florists, bands, or disc jockeys he or she can recommend?

❧ Can you see photos of previous reception setups?

❧ How many hours is the site available for? Is there a time minimum you must meet? Are there charges if the reception runs overtime?

❧ Is there free parking? If there is valet parking, what are the rates and gratuities? (If you pay for valet parking up front, post a sign informing your guests that the tip has already been paid.)

❧ Will there be coatroom and restroom attendants? A bartender? A doorman? What are the charges for these?

❧ If you've arranged for an open bar, do you have to bring the alcohol or does the site provide it?

❧ If you've arranged for a cash bar, what will the prices be?

❧ Does the facility have more than one reception site on the premises? If someone else is occupying another room at the site, will there still be adequate parking available? Is there enough space between the two rooms to ensure privacy? (You don't want your jazz quartet drowned out by the heavy metal band playing at the graduation party next door.)

❧ Will the site coordinator be available to advise you on decorations? Layout? Seating?

❧ Is there a separate room where photographs can be taken? Where can you change into your going-away clothes?

❧ Who pays for any police or security that may be required? (It is customary for a policeman to be present at public function sites where alcohol is being served.)

❧ What is the layout of the tables? How many people can sit comfortably at each table?

❧ Are the costs (room rental, catering, etc.) fixed? If not, what is the ceiling for each cost?

❧ Will your deposit be returned in the event of a cancellation?

❧ Are there any other possible reception-related charges?

Caterers

Although you and your groom will probably be too excited to eat much on your wedding day, it would be wrong to assume the same about your guests. You two will be dining on love, excitement, and romance; your guests would prefer beef, chicken, a sandwich—anything, in short, to soak up the champagne. That's where the caterer comes in.

Before you go searching for a caterer, find out what your reception site does and doesn't provide. Some sites will offer linens, glassware and dinnerware, tables, chairs—everything but the food. Others provide nothing, not even a place to sit. Know what you need ahead of time so you'll know what to look for.

Catering can be basic or complex: two people in a kitchen making sandwiches and hors d'oeuvres for an at-home reception; a traveling company complete with cooks and a wait staff, who serve you at your rented reception site; or a full-service caterer supplying tables, chairs, linens, dinnerware, and a full bar, and coordinating your whole reception for you, from flowers to photos. In between, there are a great many variations on these three approaches. The room may begin to spin as you consider the options, but if you don't want your guests' heads spinning from hunger, settle down and take stock of the situation. The type of reception and the location (along with your budget) will help you determine the kind of caterer you need; after that, all that's left is to find out who can do it best at a price you can afford.

Caterers can be friendly, inexpensive, cooperative, and every other good adjective under the sun, but if their food doesn't taste good, they'll be nothing but bad news for your reception. Don't subject your guests to rubber meatballs for the sake of a great deal. You don't have to serve an extravagant dinner of prime rib, but you do want food that's worth the money you'll pay for it. Don't hire anyone without tasting the food first; if no samples are available for you in the initial consultation, ask to sample the items you are interested in at a second consultation.

IN-HOUSE CATERERS

If you're lucky, the reception site will have an in-house caterer that fits your budget, serves great food, and knows how to work with you. All hotels offer such services, as do most country clubs. There are several advantages to an in-house caterer, the main one being that you don't have to go through the trouble of finding one yourself. The in-house caterer is already familiar with the particulars of the room, which can carry many advantages (for instance, linens and dinnerware that really complement the overall atmosphere).

But the in-house picture is not all roses. In-house catering is usually more expensive than independent catering, often charging you for lots of little extras (read: things you don't want or need) as part of one all-inclusive package. So, to get the best value, you just shop around and bring in your own people, right? Unfortunately, it's not always that simple. Some reception sites that offer catering may allow you the option of bringing in your own, but with others, it's the house band or nothing. If the food is good and the price reasonable, you may be able to live with this. However, if during your taste test you find yourself gagging on something that may be chicken (but may not be, considering that gray coloring), consider moving your reception somewhere else.

INDEPENDENT CATERERS

Independent caterers come in a number of shapes and sizes. Each offers a different degree of services; each has a different price.

"Bare-bones" caterers specialize in keeping it simple—they provide food and food only. Everything else—beverages, linens, dinnerware, glasses, and even waiters and waitresses—has to come from you. Sometimes this can work out to your advantage; these caterers may offer good food at a low price, and you can shop around to get the other elements yourself. The disadvantage, of course, is that this is very inconvenient. You're going to have to go out and do some legwork, and chances are your schedule will be pretty full already. There are businesses that specialize in renting party goods and equipment, but even if you do know the right places to shop, buying or renting everything separately can be a logistical nightmare. If your reception site doesn't provide tables and chairs, for example, you're either going to have to become an instant expert in rental furniture, or think up some fascinating party games that will keep your guests from realizing that they have to eat cross-legged on the floor.

Full-service caterers, which most people associate with a wedding reception, provide food, beverages, a wait staff, and bartenders. Most also offer linens and dinnerware. If you need tables and chairs, this type of caterer will usually do all the legwork for you and simply add that to the cost of your total bill. If you're lucky, they'll charge you exactly what the rental agency charged them, but it's not uncommon for them to add a fee for their trouble; so get a written estimate before you authorize anything. Some of these caterers will let you supply the alcohol, but others prefer not to worry about the potential liability (or their loss of liquor revenue).

There are also caterers who function much like a wedding coordinator, offering just about every item and service you could imagine, as well as a few you probably haven't. If you choose to pay their hefty fees, they'll take on the entire responsibility of planning your reception: music, flowers, photographer, the whole nine yards. This may sound like a dream come true, but this kind of service doesn't come cheap. Also, you're flying blind. How are you to know whether you'll get a high-quality photographer—or a close (amateur) friend of the chef who has a nice camera? Third (and most important) is the question of quality. With so many irons in so many fires, even seasoned veterans can make horrendous mistakes.

If you find a catering service of this type that really appeals to you, consider contracting them for the traditional catering services, but keep tight control over everything else.

Questions to Ask the Caterer

Caterers usually quote you an estimated price based on food prices at that time. About ninety days before the wedding (or perhaps later), they should give you the final price, reflecting current food rates. Early on, ask for an estimate of how much the price will change between the estimated figure and the actual cost. (You don't want to be charged $30 per meal if the estimate was $18.) Ask about any price guarantees.

No matter what type of caterer you need, there are a few key questions you should ask before you make any commitments:

- What types of meal service are offered? Sit-down? Buffet? French? Sit-down and buffet are the most common services, but at an extremely formal affair you might want French-style service. With French style, the food is brought out on large platters by waiters trained in this service. The waiters either serve each person from the platter, or hold the platter while guests serve themselves. No matter how simple or fancy the service, if you want it, you'd better make sure your caterer can deliver.

- Are there several meal options? Do they specialize in any particular cuisine?

- Is the catering service covered by insurance? If you are counting on them to provide liquor, do they have liability insurance to cover any accidents that could occur after the wedding as a result of drunk driving? (It should go without saying that the caterer must have a liquor license if liquor will be served by staff!)

- What will the ratio of staff to guests be? Will there be enough people to staff the tables? Will those people be dressed appropriately for the occasion?

- Will they make provisions for guests with special dietary needs? Try to plan ahead for guests on vegetarian, low-cholesterol, or kosher diets.

- Will meals be provided for the disc jockey (or band), photographer, and videographer? They get hungry, too.

- Does the caterer offer hors d' oeuvres? At what cost? What is the price difference between having them served by waiters and waitresses and displaying them on a buffet table?

🌸 Can the caterer provide a wedding cake? How about a dessert cart (with lots of cavity-causing desserts)? At what price?

🌸 Is there a "cake-cutting fee"? Some caterers will try to hit you with this charge (often several dollars per guest), which supposedly goes to cover the labor cost of slicing the cake, plus providing forks and plates. Never mind that you are already paying mandatory labor and gratuities fees for the staff. We strongly advise that you do your very best to negotiate your way out of this ridiculous cost.

🌸 Can you inspect linens, dinnerware, and related items beforehand? You don't want brown tablecloths unless you ask for them.

🌸 Does the caterer's fee include gratuities for the staff, or will you be hit with that bill later? What about the cost of the coatroom attendants, bartenders, and others who may be working at the reception?

🌸 What is the refund policy, in the unlikely event you should have to cancel? It's better to be safe than sorry.

🌸 What does the caterer do with leftover food? Since you're paying for it, you may wish to have it boxed up for yourself—or perhaps given to a local charity.

When you decide on a caterer who meets your budget needs and who has answered these questions to your satisfaction, get every part of your agreement in writing. Don't leave any stone unturned—you might get tripped up later.

Selecting a Menu

A sit-down meal is generally considered more formal than a buffet. In addition, many people feel they're treating their guests better by not making them stand in line for their food. Buffet service, does, however, have its advantages: it's less expensive to serve than a sit-down meal, because it eliminates the need for waiters and waitresses. A buffet meal can add a relaxed touch to a morning or afternoon wedding.

If you do decide to go with a buffet, consider having two food stations instead of one. Your guests will get to the food twice as fast, an especially nice touch if you're planning a rather large wedding. Though buffet service saves you the cost of a wait staff, it does require more food than a sit-down meal, since portions are not controlled. You will want to have plenty of food visible so that no one will feel shy about taking enough to eat. The caterer should assign a few staff members to watch the table to replace any food that starts to run low.

Semi-buffet service is another option. With this service, the tables are already set with plates, flatware, and glasses. The wait staff clear the tables and serve drinks; the only thing the guests pick up at the buffet table is the food. Since many people believe a table set with coffee cups is too "diner-like," a separate table is usually set up with cups, coffee, cream, and sugar.

Serving Drinks

The biggest controversy today surrounding alcohol and weddings is whether to have an open or cash bar. At an open bar, guests drink for free; at a cash bar, they pay for each drink. Some people will tell you that it's not polite to force your guests to pay for their drinks; after all, the argument goes, they've already spent money on shower and wedding gifts, new outfits, and baby sitters. How much more are you going to ask of them?

On the other side of the debate is the sobering (no pun intended!) fact that open bars can get extremely expensive! And consider this. With an open bar, not only will there be a lot of half-full glasses left around, there are also likely to be some pretty intoxicated people wandering around. Perhaps the biggest argument against an open bar (even if you can afford it), is that in these times of increased awareness, tougher drunk driving laws, and heavy liability issues, no one wants to endanger family and friends, or other drivers. Your best bet is to stick with a cash bar. One caveat, though; if yours is a Jewish wedding, a cash bar runs contrary to accepted ideas of Jewish hospitality. It simply isn't done.

If you still feel guilty about making your guests buy drinks, here are a few things you can do instead and still keep your costs down:

- ❧ Have an open bar for the first hour of the reception only. This will ease your guilt, help your guests pass the time pleasantly while you're off taking pictures, and minimize any problems with guests.
- ❧ Offer tray service. Your guests don't have to pay for their drinks, and you don't incur the massive expense of an open bar. How does tray service work? You choose a few drinks that you feel will be popular with the majority of your guests (include beer and wine for sure bets). The wait staff will bring these selections around on a tray and offer them to your guests. The servers do not float around with drinks all night, but serve them on a schedule to keep down costs (and over-consumption). You might send the servers around before dinner, when dinner is being served, and at other times during the course of the reception. It's wise to stop serving well before the end of the reception to give people a chance to sober up. Tray service will obviously cost you more than a cash bar, but at least you can regulate how much liquor gets consumed.
- ❧ Serve champagne punch. A punch like this is fairly light, alcohol-wise, and people just aren't likely to drink glass after glass of punch. Maybe it's an image thing.

THE SOFT STUFF

Always make sure that there are nonalcoholic options on hand for any guests who would prefer to steer clear of the hard stuff. Every bar should stock soft drinks, but you might also add a nonalcoholic punch. (Punches can also look very inviting when served in an elegant bowl or fountain.) Don't think you're restricted to that bright red stuff you drank as a kid. There are plenty of delicious nonalcoholic options, including a sparkling grape juice that looks just like champagne!

CHAMPAGNE OR SPARKLING WINE?

Though we commonly refer to any sparkling white wine as champagne, only the wine made in the Champagne region of France deserves this title. As you might expect, you'll pay more for the real thing (how does $60 or more per bottle sound)— whereas you can pick up a decent bottle of sparkling wine for around $10. Unless you have a champagne connoisseur on your guest list, nobody will know the difference, and you'll be saving yourself a bundle. If you're like most people, you'll only want enough "champagne" to fill everyone's glass once for the opening (best man's) toast. If your caterer is responsible for procuring the champagne and other liquor, all you have to worry about is the bill; if you have to buy it yourself, assume that each bottle of champagne will yield seven glasses.

UNCORKING THE CORKAGE FEE

This fee may be levied if you have your reception in a restaurant or hotel, but opt to bring your own liquor. The corkage fee is meant to make up for the loss of drink revenue; according to the management, it covers the cost of their staff uncorking and serving the drinks. If you are planning on bringing your own liquor, find out the price of the corkage fee in advance; it may be so high that it negates any savings you made by BYOBing. (Again, some establishments simply won't allow you to bring your own liquor, so this fee may not even be an issue.) Unlike the similarly absurd cake-cutting fee charged by caterers, this one's got a long tradition and is going to be difficult, if not impossible, to wiggle out of.

Reception Traditions

THE HEAD TABLE

The head table is wherever the bride and groom sit, and is, understandably, the focus of the reception. It usually faces the other tables and is near the dance floor. The table is sometimes elevated, and decorations or flowers are usually low enough to allow guests a perfect view of you and your groom.

Traditionally, honor attendants, bridesmaids, and ushers join the newlyweds at the head table. Unless the table is round, the bride and groom typically sit in the middle, with the best man next to the bride and the maid of honor next to the groom. The ushers and bridesmaids then sit alternating on both sides of the bride and groom. Child attendants should sit at a regular table with their parents.

THE FIRST TOAST

After the receiving line has ended and the wedding party and guests have been seated, everyone is served a glass of champagne or another sparkling beverage. The best man then stands up and toasts the newlyweds. The rest of the guests stand, too, but the bride and groom remain seated.

After the best man's toast, the groom may make a toast, then the bride, and then the parents, members of the wedding party, or other special guests may toast the bride and groom. All toasts except the best man's toast are strictly optional. Once the toasting is over, the dancing is started and dinner is served.

THE OPENING DANCES

The bride and groom's first dance is often one of the most romantic parts of your reception. You and your new husband dance or sway to a song the two of you have carefully chosen for its sentimental value, while your guests look on. Only the most hardened cynic can't help feeling nostalgic at the sight of a bride and groom dancing their first dance together as husband and wife.

After the first dance, the bride dances with her father, and then the groom dances with his mother. Afterwards, the bride and groom's parents dance, the bride dances with her father-in-law, the groom dances with his mother-in-law, and the brides-maids and ushers dance with each other. Then open dancing begins. Of course, you may eliminate or combine some or all of these dances if you choose, and simply have the band-leader or master of ceremonies announce that open dancing will begin immediately.

THE CAKE-CUTTING CEREMONY

Aside from being a tasty dessert, the wedding cake performs a very important function: it is the centerpiece of the ever-popular cake-cutting ceremony. This is when the bride and groom cut the first piece of cake together and feed each other a bite. In some parts of the country, this ritual is accompanied by the tune "The Farmer in the Dell," with the guests singing lyrics modified for the occasion. ("The bride cuts the cake," "The groom cuts the cake," "The bride feeds the groom," and so on.)

At a sit-down reception, the cake is cut right before the dessert (if any) is served. The caterer or baker then cuts the rest of the cake and distributes it to the guests.

THE BOUQUET AND GARTER TOSS

The bouquet and garter toss are examples of once widely accepted traditions that have gradu-ally lost favor. Today, many brides find the tradi-tion—in which the bride throws her bouquet to a group of single women, while the groom removes the garter from the bride's leg and then tosses it to a group of single men—to be . . . well, degrading. As a result, many brides decide to eliminate this tradition, in whole or in part. Others still enjoy the tradition and the fun that ensues. Whether or not you choose to include this tradition in your wedding is up to you. Remember, it's your big day.

Reception site: _____

Address: _____

_____

Telephone: _____

Contact: _____ Hours: _____

Appointments:

Date: _____ Time: _____

Date: _____ Time: _____

Date: _____ Time: _____

Date: _____ Time: _____

Cost:

Total amount due: _____

Amount of deposit: _____ Date: _____

Balance due: _____ Date: _____

Room reserved: _____

Date: _____ Time: _____ Number of hours: ____

Overtime cost: _____

Occupancy: _____

Final head count due date: _____

Reception location includes the following services: _____

_____

Reception location includes the following equipment: _____

_____

Terms of cancellation: _____

_____

Other: _____

Item	Description	Cost	Notes
RECEPTION SITE			
Site rental			
Overtime fee			
Other			
EQUIPMENT			
Tent			
Chairs			
Tables			
Linens			
Other			
SERVICE			
Servers			
Bartenders			
Valet parking attendants			
Coat checkers			
Other			
OTHER (LIST BELOW)			
TOTAL			

Name (if different from reception site): _____

Address: _____

Telephone: _____

Contact: _____ Hours: _____

Appointments:

Date: _____ Time: _____

Date: _____ Time: _____

Date: _____ Time: _____

Date of hired services: _____ Time: _____

Number of hours: _____ Cocktail hour: _____

Overtime cost: _____ Final head count due date: _____

Menu: _____

_____

Sit down or buffet? _____

Includes the following services: _____

_____

Includes the following equipment: _____

_____

Cost:

Total amount due: _____

Amount of deposit: _____ Date: _____

Balance due: _____ Date: _____

Gratuities included? ❑ Yes ❑ No Sales tax included? ❑ Yes ❑ No

Terms of cancellation: _____

_____

Notes: _____

_____

Item	Description	Cost	Notes
FOOD			
Appetizers			
Entrees			
Dessert			
Other food			
BEVERAGES			
Nonalcoholic			
Champagne			
Wine			
Liquor			
EQUIPMENT			
Tent			
Chairs			
Tables			
Linens			
Dinnerware			
Flatware			
Glassware			
Serving pieces			
Other			
SERVICE			
Servers			
Bartenders			
Valet parking attendants			
Coat checkers			
Overtime cost			
OTHER			
GRATUITIES			
SALES TAX			
TOTAL			

Food	Description	Number	Cost
Appetizers			
Entrees			
Desserts (if any)			
Beverages (nonalcoholic)			
Wine			
Champagne			
Open bar			
Other			
Gratuities			
Sales tax			
TOTAL			

Name of rental company: _____

Address: _____

_____

Telephone: _____

Contact: _____

Hours: _____

Order date: _____

Delivery? Pick up? (circle one) _____

Date: _____ Time: _____

Special instructions: _____

Total amount due: _____

Amount of deposit: _____ Date: _____

Balance due: _____ Date _____

Cancellation policy: _____

_____

_____

Damaged goods policy: _____

_____

_____

Notes: _____

_____

_____

_____

_____

_____

_____

Item	Description	Quantity	Cost	Total Cost (Quantity x Cost)
CEREMONY EQUIPMENT				
Aisle runner				
Candelabra				
Canopy/Chuppah				
Lattice arch				
Microphone				
Other				
TENTS				
Size				
Size				
Flooring/Carpeting				
Lighting				
Decoration				
Other				
CHAIRS				
Style				
Style				
Style				
Other				
TABLES				
Size				
Size				
Size				
Other				

Item	Description	Quantity	Cost	Total Cost (Quantity x Cost)
LINENS				
Table				
Chair covers				
Napkins				
Other				
DINNERWARE				
Dinner plates				
Salad plates				
Bread plates				
Dessert plates				
Cake plates				
Soup bowls				
Fruit bowls				
Cups and saucers				
Other				
FLATWARE				
Dinner forks				
Salad forks				
Dinner knives				
Steak knives				
Butter knives				
Spoons				
Soup spoons				
Serving spoons				
Meat forks				

Item	Description	Quantity	Cost	Total Cost (Quantity x Cost)
Carving knives				
Cake serving set				
Other				
GLASSWARE				
Wine glasses				
Champagne glasses				
Water goblets				
Highball glasses				
Double rocks glasses				
Snifters				
16 oz. glasses				
8 oz. glasses				
Punch cups				
Other				
BAR EQUIPMENT				
Ice buckets				
Ice tubs				
Bottle/can openers				
Corkscrews				
Cocktail shakers				
Stirring sticks				
Electric blenders				
Strainers				
Cocktail napkins				
Other				

Item	Description	Quantity	Cost	Total Cost (Quantity x Cost)
SERVING PIECES				
Serving trays				
Platters				
Serving bowls				
Punch bowls				
Water pitchers				
Salt and pepper sets				
Butter dishes				
Creamer/sugar sets				
Bread baskets				
Condiment trays				
Other				
MISCELLANEOUS				
Coffee maker				
Insulated coffee pitchers				
Hot plates				
Microwaves				
Grill				
Coolers				
Coat racks				
Hangers				
Ash trays				
Trash cans				
Other				
TOTAL				

Draw a simple, aerial-view diagram of the reception hall below. It should include the head table, parents' tables, guest tables, and any other significant features of the room (dance floor, bar, location of band or DJ, exits, etc.).

Head Table:

Shape of table:

Number of chairs:

Order of seating (list or draw diagram below):

Bride's Parents' Table:

Shape of table:

Number of chairs:

Order of seating (list or draw diagram below):

Groom's Parents' Table:

Shape of table:

Number of chairs:

Order of seating (list or draw diagram below):

Guest Tables:

Shape of tables:

_____

Average number of chairs per table:

_____

Total number of guests:

_____

Table Number _____   **Table Number** _____
Name of Guest: **Name of Guest:**

_____   _____

_____   _____

_____   _____

_____   _____

_____   _____

_____   _____

_____   _____

_____   _____

Table Number _____
Name of Guest:

_____
_____
_____
_____
_____
_____
_____
_____
_____

Table Number _____
Name of Guest:

_____
_____
_____
_____
_____
_____
_____
_____
_____

Table Number _____
Name of Guest:

_____
_____
_____
_____
_____
_____
_____
_____
_____

Table Number _____
Name of Guest:

_____
_____
_____
_____
_____
_____
_____
_____
_____

Table Number _____
Name of Guest:

_____

_____

_____

_____

_____

_____

_____

_____

_____

_____

Table Number _____
Name of Guest:

_____

_____

_____

_____

_____

_____

_____

_____

_____

_____

Table Number _____
Name of Guest:

_____

_____

_____

_____

_____

_____

_____

_____

_____

_____

Table Number _____
Name of Guest:

_____

_____

_____

_____

_____

_____

_____

_____

_____

_____

Give a copy of this checklist to your Reception Site Coordinator and Band Leader or Disc Jockey.

Introduce entire bridal party? ❑ Yes ❑ No Music: _____

Introduce only bride and groom? ❑ Yes ❑ No Music: _____

Parent(s) of bride: _____

Parent(s) of groom: _____

Grandparent(s) of bride: _____

Grandparent(s) of groom: _____

Flower girl(s): _____

Ring bearer(s): _____

Bridesmaids: _____ Ushers: _____

_____

_____

_____

_____

_____

Maid of honor: _____ Best man: _____

Matron of honor: _____

Bride's first name: _____ Groom's first name: _____

Bride and groom as they are to be introduced: _____

_____

Receiving line at reception? ❑ Yes ❑ No When: _____

Music: _____

Blessing? ❑ Yes ❑ No By Whom: _____

First toast? ❑ Yes ❑ No By Whom: _____

Other toasts? ❑ Yes ❑ No By Whom: _____

By Whom: _____

By Whom: _____

First dance: ❑ Yes ❑ No   When: _____

_____ Music: _____

To join in first dance: _____

Maid of honor and best man? ❑ Yes ❑ No _____

Parents of bride and groom? ❑ Yes ❑ No _____

Bridesmaids and ushers? ❑ Yes ❑ No _____

Guests? ❑ Yes ❑ No _____

Father-daughter dance? ❑ Yes ❑ No Music: _____

Mother-son dance? ❑ Yes ❑ No Music: _____

Open dance floor for guests after first dance? ❑ Yes ❑ No _____

Cake cutting? ❑ Yes ❑ No   Music: _____

Bouquet toss? ❑ Yes ❑ No _____

Garter toss? ❑ Yes ❑ No _____

Last dance? ❑ Yes ❑ No   Music: _____

Other event: _____

When: _____ Music: _____

Other event: _____

When: _____ Music: _____

Special requests and dedications: _____

_____

_____

_____

_____

_____

Notes: _____

_____

CHAPTER TWELVE

WEDDING PHOTOGRAPHY AND VIDEOGRAPHY

"A picture paints a thousand words." At no time in your life will this statement seem more appropriate than on your wedding day. You'll be feeling things you can't even recognize, never mind describe. And thanks to the art of photography and videography, you won't have to. A good set of wedding prints and a wedding video will go a long way toward capturing and preserving all the emotions, excitement, and memories for you and your family.

Hiring a Wedding Photographer

Good photography is not just clicking on the auto-focus and shooting away with the family Instamatic. It's an art requiring skill and planning. Needless to say, you don't want to put this huge responsibility in the hands of just anyone; so be very careful about whom you choose. Beware of "professional" photographers who really aren't. Imagine how you'd feel after finding out the entire ceremony was photographed with the lens cap on—a drastic example, but not unheard of. There are countless stories of couples who have received less than quality work for their money—photos that are blurry, ill-composed, and made up of colors that don't appear in the natural world, and definitely didn't appear at the wedding, or shots of family and friends with demonic red dots in their eyes. Take the time to find a photographer who will do you and your wedding justice.

Only work with a reputable photographer—there is no substitute for the education and experience of a professional. Finding such a professional may not be that easy, however. It's quite common for the best people to be booked a year or more in advance, so begin your search early. Start with the word-of-mouth approach: ask your friends, family, coworkers, or anyone else you know who's been married or coordinated a wedding recently. Their opinions and their wedding albums will go a long way toward helping you find some options.

Be sure to ask about their overall experience with the photographer or studio in question. The pictures may have come out like a dream, but the person behind the lens could have been a nightmare: rude, pushy, sloppy. If that's the case, keep looking. Your aim is to hire someone who takes great photographs, and does so in a way that makes everyone feel at ease. If you've ever been to a wedding where the photographer has fallen drunk into the punch bowl or made a pass at the maid of honor, you already know that you don't want this happening to you.

You're looking for someone who makes you feel comfortable, someone who is willing to work with you every step of the way. A good photographer who relates well with you, your groom, and your families can bring out the best in everyone and preserve it forever on film.

It also goes without saying that you're looking for someone who's very talented. How can you assess the photographer's talent if you don't even know how to load film into a camera? For starters, look for crispness and thoughtful composition. Did the photographer make good use of lighting? Were a variety of backgrounds and settings used, or is everyone always standing in front of the cake? Is there a good balance of formal and candid shots? This should give you an idea of what to look for, but if you have a friend or family member who knows photography, ask him or her to help you evaluate possible photographers.

In addition to the look of the photographs, find out how the photographer will process them. Many studios these days use chemical laboratories for color processing, but this method pales (no pun intended) beside an artist processing the colors by hand. With this method, colors are much more accurate, and the details are plentiful and clear. If this sounds suspiciously like an expensive route to go, it is, but if you can put aside the extra money in your photography budget, it's also the best route to take.

If you can't find a good photographer by word of mouth, go to some bridal fairs and photography shows. Both places are likely to yield plenty of good candidates.

When interviewing photographers who haven't worked with anyone you know, make sure you get references and closely examine their work. The photos in the portfolio may be wonderful, but it is possible that the person you're talking to bought them from someone else, and in real life doesn't know an f-stop from a truck stop! Ask for the names of former clients that you can contact to get another customer's point of view.

In the end, you must make your choice based on the individual's talent, your own ceremony and reception needs, your budget, and your gut feeling about the person you'll be working with. Until you sit down with the photographer to map out a battle plan for the wedding, you will probably be dealing with price ranges rather than concrete amounts. The final price will depend on the approach to the wedding you develop with the photographer. Get the best value you can, but you will do yourself a big favor by opting to pay a little more for a quality job.

Cost

Some studios will charge you a basic hourly rate. Others charge a flat fee based on the photographer's time and a certain number of photographs, such as seven hours of work and a thirty-six-picture album. Studios may also charge for the photographer's travel time, or for overtime if the job runs longer than expected.

The complete fee for a photographer typically ranges from $500 to $2,000, depending upon the quality, type, and number of photographs. Get the exact fee in advance. You want to make sure you're not signing on for more than you can handle.

Be sure to find out what the prices are for any additional photos you may want to order beyond the original package. The studio may have given you a very reasonable price for your package, but may charge $100 for every extra photo. Some studios include albums, frames, and special parents' books as part of the deal; ask if yours does too.

Also, be sure to ask whether the studio will hang on to your negatives, and if so, for how long. If for some reason you should want or need a picture from the wedding months or years later, you'll want to know how to get one made. Most studios will only keep the negatives for a few years; if having them forever is important to you, ask about buying them.

Consumer Alert

A photographer's high price tag does not necessarily mean you'll be getting high quality. A low price tag, however, is a pretty reliable sign that you're likely to see low-quality results. Photography is one of the parts of your wedding you should try not to skimp on. You probably won't be dragging your wedding dress out of storage very often, and you may not even remember what kind of flowers you carried, but you can bet that you and your loved ones will be going back to your wedding photographs time and time again. So when choosing your wedding photographer, you should:

- Steer clear of part-time photographers who only occasionally handle weddings. They are not likely to have the equipment and experience of an expert in the field.
- Make sure the studio you choose specializes in weddings. You may love the studio that did your high school graduation picture, but if portraits are all they do, they'll probably flunk out at your wedding. Only experienced wedding photographers know all the nuances of photographing a wedding: the potential problems (and how to avoid them); when to fade into the background when working in a crowd; and the best way to compose a moment.
- Be sure to get every part of the agreement with your photographer in writing. Include the date, the agreed-upon arrival time, the length of shooting time, estimates for additional fees or overtime charges, the cost of the package you've selected, and anything else of importance. You don't want to be hit with unexpected bills after the fact.
- Avoid very large studios that appear to use the assembly-line approach. Often they employ as many as a hundred photographers and won't guarantee which one will show up on your wedding day, or how qualified he or she is to do the job. Always ask to see sample wedding photos that were

taken by the same photographer who will be working your wedding. If the studio can't or won't supply them, find another one to work with.

Working with Your Photographer

After you've chosen the photographer, sit down with him or her and map out your photographic wants, needs, and expectations. It's important to establish a good relationship with your photographer well before the wedding so that everyone feels comfortable when the big (and usually nerve-racking) day comes around.

Ask how many pictures the photographer plans to take on your wedding day. A good-quality studio will take three times as many as you signed up for, to give you the best and broadest selection. If you asked for the thirty-six-photo album, you certainly don't want the photographer to take only thirty-six pictures.

As you'll soon find out, there are certain standard poses that are traditionally taken, so be sure to tell the photographer if you have additional ideas in mind to be captured on film. Give him or her a list (see the Photograph Checklist at the end of this chapter) of all the special people you want pictures of, especially people outside of the wedding party. Your photographer may be exceptional, but he or she is probably not a mind-reader. If your eighty-year-old aunt is famous for her rendition of the Twist at family functions, make sure you tell the photographer you want that moment on film! Similarly, if you don't want some of the standard poses (groom with his ushers, groom with bridal attendants, etc.), let the photographer know. Why waste time or film on pictures you don't want?

Photographic Extras

Aside from working with you on the wedding day, you may want the photographer to take an engagement photo and/or a formal bridal portrait. If so, you'll want to iron out the details with the photographer in your initial meeting.

The popularity of bridal portraits is not what it used to be. Salons have trouble getting the gown ready in enough time to take the portrait, so if you know you really want one, iron out those details in advance. Most brides have a portrait taken as a gift to their parents, but the photo can also be used as part of a wedding announcement in the newspaper. If you plan to send a copy along to the paper, be sure to order a 5" by 7" black and white shot from the photographer.

Bridal portraits are usually taken either at the photographer's studio or at the bridal salon on the last day of your fitting. Most photographers will meet you at the salon, but you should double-check to make sure.

For your bridal portrait, you will need:

- Your gown
- A hat, veil, or any other headpiece you select
- Gloves, if you will be wearing them
- Wedding shoes and stockings
- Any jewelry you plan to wear on your wedding day
- A silk bridal bouquet (borrowed from your florist, a bridal salon, or a photography studio)

If your photography budget is overflowing with extra funds, you might consider thank-you notes that feature a picture of you and your groom. You can get one standard photo that goes on every note, or, if you're really ambitious, you can personalize each one with a photo of you opening the person's gift. These photo-notes are not common practice, but they do add a personal touch and hint at a little extra effort on your part.

Photography Options and Trends

FORMAL PHOTOS BEFORE THE WEDDING

Although it is considered bad luck for the groom to see the bride before the ceremony, many couples today feel comfortable doing away with this superstition and taking the formal shots before the wedding. Handling the formal photo session this way makes life easier for a lot of people: the photographer doesn't have to rush to get all the shots on your list before hungry guests start a riot; the guests don't suffer from starvation or boredom while they wait for you to pose, pose, and pose again; and you and the wedding party get to enjoy more of the reception.

If seeing the groom before the ceremony is absolutely out of the question for you, try to take as many pictures as you can without him—you alone, you and your parents, you and your attendants, and so on. At the reception, speed things up by making sure everyone who's going to be in a picture knows where he or she is supposed to be.

SHOOTING ON LOCATION

Some couples opt to take their formal wedding photos at a location other than the reception site. Sometimes the spot they select is of great sentimental value—and sometimes it's chosen just because the scenery is gorgeous.

Here are some on-location photo-shoot suggestions:

- At a beach, lake, or garden (in the spring and summer)
- Near foliage (in the fall)
- In a snow-covered wood (in the winter)

If you do plan to take your photo shoot on the road, remember that your guests will have to wait even longer than usual to see you (and their dinner) at the reception. As a way to ease their impatience (and their stomachs), consider offering a first-hour open bar and serving some hors d' oeuvres.

BLACK AND WHITE PHOTOGRAPHS

Though you may associate black and white photos with your parents' and grandparent's weddings, they can add a special touch to yours, too! Color may be brilliant, but black and white is classic. It creates atmosphere and style. Black and white lends itself best to formal portraits; it gives them a timeless feel. For candid and action shots, though, it's best to stay with color. How can you show off your ability to color-coordinate the flowers, the dresses, and the cake without color photos to pass around?

For a really distinctive look, the studio can add some hand-colored tinting to your black and white photos—the same process that was used for movie star stills in the 1940s. If you thought you felt special on your wedding day, imagine how you'll feel seeing you and your groom looking like the silver screen's greatest lovers!

Of course while you're adding all this style and atmosphere, remember to add a little more money to your overall bill. As odd as it may seem, black and white photos (even the untinted variety) cost more than color. While proofs for color shots can be processed by machine, all processing for black and white shots must be done by hand. Some studios will charge you an additional fee for each roll of black and white film shot; others add on a flat amount meant to cover the whole job.

DISPOSABLE CAMERAS

Some of the best photos from your wedding may not even come from the photographer. Place a disposable camera (the kind sold at tourist spots and drugstores) on each table, with a note asking your guests to click away at the people and action around them during the reception. Collect the cameras at the end of the reception and you'll have lots of wonderful candids of people and events the photographer probably wouldn't dream of shooting—and at a fraction of the cost.

Name of photographer/studio:

Address:

Telephone:

Contact:

Hours they can be reached:

Directions:

Appointments:

Date: Time:

Date: Time:

Date: Time:

Name of package (if applicable):

Date of hired services: Time:

Number of hours: Overtime cost:

Travel fee:

Fee for custom pages:

Fee for black and white prints:

Fee for sepia prints:

Fee for album inscription:

Additional fees (if any):

Engagement session included? ❑ Yes ❑ No   Additional cost, if any:

Will attend rehearsal? ❑ Yes ❑ No   Additional cost, if any:

Cost of film, proofing, and processing included? ❑ Yes ❑ No

Additional cost, if any:

Type of wedding album included:

Date proofs will be ready:

Date order will be ready:

Additional services included:

Cost:

Total amount due:

Amount of deposit: Date:

Balance due: Date:

Sales tax included? ❏ Yes ❏ No

Terms of cancellation:

Notes:

Included in Package:

Item	Number Included in Package	Cost of Each Additional	Notes
8" x 10" engagement portraits			
5" x 7" engagement prints			
4" x 5" engagement prints			
Wallet size engagement prints			
Wedding proofs			
Wallet size prints			
3 ½" x 5" prints			
4" x 5" prints			
5" x 7" prints			
8" x 10" prints			
11" x 14" portraits			
Other prints (list below)			
Preview album			
Wedding album			
Wedding album pages			
Parent albums			
Other (list below)			

Photograph Checklist

Give a copy of this completed form to your wedding photographer.

Name of bride and groom: _____

Address: _____

_____

Telephone: _____

Wedding date: _____

Ceremony location: _____

Reception location: _____

Special instructions: _____

_____

_____

_____

_____

Portraits:

❑ You and the groom during the ceremony (if possible)
❑ An official wedding portrait of you and your groom
❑ The entire wedding party
❑ You, your groom, and family members
❑ You and your mother
❑ You and your father
❑ You with both parents
❑ You with your groom's parents (your new in-laws)
❑ The groom with his mother
❑ The groom with his father
❑ The groom with both parents
❑ The groom with your parents (his new in-laws)
❑ Combination photos of the attendants
❑ You and your groom with any special people in your lives, such as grandparents or godparents
❑ Other:

Photos from the ceremony (if possible):
❑ Each member of the wedding party as he or she comes down the aisle
❑ The mother of the bride as she is ushered down the aisle
❑ The groom's parents
❑ You and your father coming down the aisle
❑ Your father leaving you at the altar
❑ The wedding party at the altar
❑ The ring exchange
❑ The vows
❑ The lighting of any candles or special ceremony features
❑ Any relatives or friends who participate in the ceremony by doing a reading or lighting a candle
❑ The kiss
❑ The walk from the altar
❑ Other:

Candids:
❑ Getting ready for the ceremony; putting on the veil, the garter
❑ The bridesmaids, and you with them before the wedding
❑ You and your father leaving
❑ You and your father arriving at the ceremony
❑ Getting out of the limousine/car
❑ You and your groom getting in the car
❑ Toasting one another in the car
❑ Reception arrival
❑ The first dance
❑ The cutting of the cake
❑ Tossing the bouquet
❑ Removing/tossing the garter
❑ Going-away dance
❑ Leaving for the honeymoon (possibly with a "just married" sign on the car)
❑ Other:

The Pros and Cons of Wedding Videos

Despite the clear and present danger of winding up on one of
those embarrassing home video shows, videotaping your wedding is
pretty much a given these days. Many couples consider their wedding video more valuable than their wedding photographs. This may
be because the bride and groom are, ironically, the two people who
usually remember the least about their wedding. They're in a fog of
emotion and excitement, and hundreds of sensory impressions go
by in a blur. Still photographs will show them a few staged poses
and how things looked; a videotape will show how things were.

Unlike a still camera, the video camera records not just images
but time—taking in all the sound and action of a scene. Rather than
focusing in on a few key friends and family members, video can
capture everybody. You can have a record of the guests as they
sing, dance, eat, fight, kiss, cry, and laugh. When a bride and
groom finally sit down to watch their videotape, it will certainly
bring back wonderful memories, but it will also show them many
things they hadn't seen before.

Hiring a Videographer

When searching for a videographer, apply the same basic guidelines
you would for a still photographer. The pictures may be moving this
time, but the images should still be crisp and clear, and the colors
should be correct. You want to be comfortable with your videographer, and confident that he won't be ordering your guests in and
out of a shot as though he were Martin Scorcese.

Don't have your wedding videotaped by a friend or relative
unless you've seen a sample of his or her work and were
impressed by it. Your groom's brother may have the best intentions
and even own a good video camera, but odds are he won't have
the necessary sound and editing equipment to make a tape for pos-
terity. He may miss some key moments if he gets caught up in the
excitement. And do you really want those choppy shots of the floor
tiles taken while he was leaping to catch the garter?

The videographer should have up-to-date, quality equipment, not a twenty-five-year-old Super 8 camera. Also ask about editing and dubbing machines, microphones, and lights. Find out how many cameras he or she has, and how many people will be assisting on the job. Some video formats require the simultaneous use of two cameras; one person with one camera will bring you up short.

Ask to view sample tapes. You're looking for smooth editing, clear sound, and an overall professional feel to the tape. With all of the technology today, you don't have to settle for anything short of broadcast-quality production values.

If you're lucky, the people at your photography studio will also offer video services. If not, perhaps they could recommend someone. And don't forget your most precious resource in these situations: word of mouth. Friends, relations, and coworkers should be able to help out with some referrals.

Once you've found someone and verified his or her references, get a written contract stipulating costs, services, labor commitments, the date, the time, and the place.

Cost

The typical wedding video package costs anywhere between $500 and $1500, depending on the quality of the equipment, the number of hours of coverage, the number of cameras, the amount of editing, and other factors. There are some very elaborate video formats out there, some featuring special lenses and special effects. You could get an Oscar-caliber videotape, but it won't come cheap. As always, remember what's most important to you, determine what you can afford, and go from there.

Types of Wedding Videos

There are two basic types of video formats available today. By far the least expensive (and least complicated) is one that uses a single camera. The action is captured by one camera, and there is no editing after the fact. What the camera saw is what you get, even if it is boring (which it often will be). But don't knock this format if it's all you can afford. You'll still have everything you want on tape. Remember, as long as you have fresh batteries in your remote control, you can use the fast-forward to your heart's content.

A more expensive option is one in which two or more cameras are used. Depending upon the talent and equipment of your videographer, you can also add in photo montages, prerecorded music, and titles. Needless to say, editing is necessary in this case, and the more specialties you get, the more you'll pay.

Some couples like the opening scenes of their videotape to feature photos of the two of them as babies, as children, with their families, and during their courtship. After this introduction comes the wedding itself. This is sometimes referred to as the "nostalgic" video style.

Another popular option has the videographer record only the events of your wedding day, in a storybook fashion. This type of video, sometimes referred to as the "documentary" style, records everything, from getting ready before the ceremony to the time when you leave the reception. The videographer may also ask members of the wedding party and guests to say a few words to you and your groom. The guests may or may not appreciate being put on the spot, but there's no reason you and the groom should be the only ones auditioning for *America's Funniest Home Videos*!

Above all, keep in mind that because videotaping is dependent on technology, there are always new techniques and equipment being advanced. What was not available for a friend's wedding last year might be commonplace today. Be sure to ask your videographer about all the options.

Name of videographer/studio:

Address:

Telephone:

Contact:

Hours they can be reached:

Directions:

Appointments:

Date: Time:

Date: Time:

Date: Time:

Name of package (if applicable):

Date of hired services: Time:

Number of hours:

Number of cameras:

Overtime cost:

Travel fee:

Additional fees (if any):

Will attend rehearsal?   ❑ Yes   ❑ No   Additional cost, if any:

Length of videotape:

Date tape will be ready:

Videotape will include:

Prewedding preparations: ❑ Yes   ❑ No

Notes:

Individual interviews with bride and groom prior to ceremony: ❑ Yes ❑ No

Notes:

Ceremony: ❑ Yes ❑ No Notes:

Reception: ❑ Yes ❑ No Notes:

Photo montage: ❑ Yes ❑ No Notes:

Other:

Package includes:

Sound: ❑ Yes ❑ No Notes:

Music: ❑ Yes ❑ No Notes:

Unedited version of wedding events: ❑ Yes ❑ No Notes:

Edited version of wedding events: ❑ Yes ❑ No Notes:

Price of additional copies of videotape:

Other:

Additional services included:

Cost:

Total amount due:

Amount of deposit: Date:

Balance due: Date:

Sales tax included? ❑ Yes ❑ No

Terms of cancellation:

Notes:

CHAPTER THIRTEEN

RECEPTION MUSIC

Reception music and entertainment can often determine the tone of the whole party. You may have planned a very elegant evening reception complete with free-flowing champagne and lobster Thermidor for dinner, but if the band starts playing Guns N' Roses covers during the cocktail hour, the romantic evening you've dreamed of will most likely be soured a bit.

You should be sure that your band or DJ can play an inclusive song list that covers a broad spectrum of musical tastes: some slow tunes, some dance tunes, some rock, some soul. You and your friends may be huge Madonna fans, but chances are your grandmother and mother-in-law are not. Different styles of music will keep everyone happy; and who knows, by the end of the evening, your mother may even join in the Electric Slide.

Setting the Right Mood

The size, formality, and budget of your wedding should help to determine the type of entertainment you have at the reception. A string quartet adds an elegant touch to a large, formal affair, while a band or disc jockey is a good choice for a lively Saturday evening celebration. If you're having your reception in a private home or a backyard, homemade tapes piped through a good stereo system will provide plenty of music to dance to. A pianist or roaming violinists may be the perfect choice for a small, romantic wedding.

Live Bands Versus DJs

These days, the big musical decision is whether to have a band or a DJ. When it comes to price, a band is definitely more expensive, but there are other factors that may influence your choice. Keep in mind that the best bands are often booked a year in advance, and DJs are often booked six to eight months ahead, so you'll want to start shopping around as soon as possible.

Live Bands

Assuming you can find a charismatic singer and talented, enthusiastic musicians, there is nothing that can match the excitement and spirit of a live band. If you're lucky enough to find a band that will work within your budget, snap them up quickly before they sign a record deal and leave town for their world tour.

If you're not so lucky, the word-of-mouth approach is usually reliable. Ask friends, relatives, and coworkers; perhaps they've thrown a wedding recently or have attended one where the music impressed them. Most of the better bands don't advertise, so word of mouth is probably your only chance to hear about them. If you still come up empty, talk to your reception site coordinator. He or she has probably seen a lot of musical entertainment come and go, and may be able to recommend someone who fits your needs. Another option is to ask around at music stores, the music departments of local colleges, or local musician's associations.

Get an earful of a number of bands. When you find one that strikes your fancy, go back and listen to them again. Some bands will impress you the first time, but may sound like a bunch of cats fighting in a garbage can on an off night. You don't want your reception to be one of their off nights.

In addition to the band's sound, look for a variety of musical styles and tempos in their repertoire. Do they play seven slow songs, one fast number, and two more slow ones—or do they know how to vary the pace? Do they appear to be enjoying themselves— or do they look like someone is holding a gun to their heads?

HIRING A BAND

Once you find a band you like, sit down and talk about exactly what you want from them before committing yourself to anything. Give them a list of songs you would like to hear at your wedding. If they don't know the songs already, will they learn them in time? Ask about their sound system and equipment needs. If your reception site is too small, or doesn't have the proper electrical outlets and fuse power, it's better to know this before you hire the band.

At most weddings, the bandleader doubles as the master of ceremonies. If you want your bandleader to perform this duty, find out whether he or she will be willing, and if any extra cost is involved. Make sure that this person has the poise and charisma to handle the responsibility; you don't want the microphone in the hands of someone who will insult your guests or make bad jokes as you cut the cake!

When you've found the perfect band and worked out all the details, you'll need to sign a contract. But before you sign it, make sure it stipulates the following:

- *The names of the band members.* This ensures that the band that you hired is the one that will show up at your wedding.
- *The band's attire.* You don't want them showing up at a formal wedding in ripped jeans and gym shorts.
- *The band's arrival time.* Make sure the band will be set up with instruments tuned before the guests arrive. The band's sound check will probably not make for soothing dinner music.
- *The exact cost of hiring the band—and everything that the price includes.* Some bands will charge you if they have to add an extra piece of equipment; others will charge a fee for playing requests. Find out in advance about everything you'll be expected to pay for.
- *The exact location of the reception.* There have actually been instances where the musical talent has shown up at the right hotel, but in the wrong city!

Disc Jockeys

Disc jockeys are fast becoming the wedding music option of choice. DJs can provide more variety than a band, they give you the original version of a song, and they're less of a logistical headache. DJs are seen as slightly less formal than bands, but they're also considerably less expensive, which adds a great deal to their appeal.

Like popular bands, many good DJs don't advertise, so finding one can be tricky. The word-of-mouth method usually works best. Perhaps you particularly enjoyed the entertainment provided at a wedding you recently attended. If so, call the bride and ask for a referral. Barring that, ask your wedding coordinator or reception site manager for some suggestions.

HIRING A DISC JOCKEY

It's important to see and hear a disc jockey in action. Look for the same things you would look for in a band: balance, variety, a good mix of fast and slow songs, a good personality, and first-rate equipment. Could this person perform the duties of master of ceremonies? Is this included in the total cost?

Find out how big his or her CD collection is; your disc jockey should be able to accommodate the majority of your guest's requests. Provide a list of what you want played at the wedding. If some of the music you want isn't available, would the DJ be willing to purchase it? More importantly, would you be charged for the trips to the music store?

As with a band, ask about the exact costs, including any possible extras. Make sure your disc jockey knows the time, the place, the address, and the proper dress. And, of course, be sure to get all the details in writing.

Some Reception Favorites

There are a few standards that are played as part of the traditional events—the bride's dance with her father, the groom's dance with his mother, the cutting of the cake, and so on—that take place at the reception. You should also be prepared to hear plenty of love songs.

Here are some reception favorites (and the people who made them famous):

"Always," Starpoint
"As Time Goes By," Irving Berlin
"Because You Loved Me," Céline Dion
"Beginnings," Chicago
"Butterfly Kisses," Bob Carlisle
"Could I Have This Dance," Anne Murray
"Daddy's Little Girl," Burke and Gerlach

"Endless Love," Diana Ross and Lionel Ritchie
"Everything I Do I Do for You," Bryan Adams
"Here and Now," Luther Vandross
"Here, There, and Everywhere," The Beatles
"Hopelessly Devoted to You," Olivia Newton-John

"If You Really Love a Woman," Bryan Adams

"I Love You So," Andy Williams

"I Will Always Love You," Whitney Houston

"I Won't Last a Day Without You," Andy Williams

"Inspiration," Chicago

"Just Because," Anita Baker

"Just the Two of Us," Grover Washington

"Just the Way You Are," Billy Joel

"Lady Love," Lou Rawls

"Misty," Johnny Mathis

"On the Wings of Love," Jeffrey Osborne

"The Power of Love," Céline Dion

"Pretty Woman," Roy Orbison

"Ribbon in the Sky," Stevie Wonder

"September Morn," Neil Diamond

"Silly Love Songs," Paul McCartney

"Sunrise, Sunset," from *Fiddler on the Roof*

"The Glory of Love," Peter Cetera

"The Wedding Song," Paul Stookey

"The Wind Beneath My Wings," Bette Midler

"Through the Eyes of Love," Melissa Manchester

"Time in a Bottle," Jim Croce

"Truly," Lionel Ritchie

"Unchained Melody," Righteous Brothers

"Unforgettable," Nat King Cole (or with Natalie Cole)

"Up Where We Belong," Joe Cocker and Jennifer Warnes

"Waiting for a Girl Like You," Foreigner

"We've Only Just Begun," The Carpenters

"Woman," John Lennon

"Wonderful Tonight," Eric Clapton

"You Are the Sunshine of My Life," Stevie Wonder

A Little Ethnic Flair

To add some spice to the usual bag of "wedding" songs, consider featuring some music from your ethnic heritage. If either you or your fiancé is Polish, for instance, play some polkas; if one of you is Italian, a couple of tarantellas are bound to light up the dance floor. If your guests have strong ethnic ties, they'll appreciate the nostalgia; guests of a different culture will enjoy learning something new.

Reception Music Worksheet

(See also the Reception Events Worksheet in Chapter 11.)

Name of band/DJ:

Address:

Telephone:

Manager/contact:

Hours he or she can be reached:

Number of performers:

Description of act:

Demo tape available?　❏ Yes　❏ No

Notes:

View live performance?　❏ Yes　❏ No

Date:　　　　Time:　　　　Location:

Appointments:

Date:　　　　　　　　Time:

Date:　　　　　　　　Time:

Date:　　　　　　　　Time:

Date of hired services:　　　　Time:

Number of hours:

Cocktail hour:

Overtime cost:

Includes the following services:

Equipment provided: _____

_____

_____

_____

_____

Equipment rented: _____

_____

_____

_____

_____

Rental costs: _____

_____

_____

_____

Cost:

Total amount due: _____

Amount of deposit: _____ Date: _____

Balance due: _____ Date: _____

Terms of cancellation: _____

_____

_____

Notes: _____

_____

_____

_____

_____

CHAPTER FOURTEEN

WEDDING
FLOWERS

For many women, flowers are the ultimate symbol of love. The beauty, the fragrance, and the spirit of flowers have captivated the female heart throughout history. Men, however, tend to consider flowers the ultimate pain in the neck. (After all, if flowers did not exist, men couldn't get in hot water for forgetting to send them.)

These two diametrically opposed views will probably continue to make flowers a bone of contention between men and women for all eternity. But there is one occasion when both men and women agree on the necessity of flowers: their wedding day. Who can say why this is? Perhaps it's because a wedding can bring out the romantic in even the most cynical of grooms. Perhaps the beauty of the day opens his eyes to the beauty of flowers. Then again, perhaps no groom wants to spend his wedding night sleeping on the floor.

Selecting a Florist

Start searching for a florist at least three months before the wedding. If you're planning to marry around Christmas or Valentine's Day, when flowers can get pretty scarce, you'll need to be sure you've chosen your florist up to six months before the date. (Unfortunately, flowers tend to be more expensive at these times of year.)

As with everything else, word of mouth is the best way to find someone reliable. If you have trouble getting good referrals from friends, consult the Yellow Pages or visit florists' booths at area wedding expositions. Ask for photos of previous displays the florist has done; check references to make sure there is a history of quality work for actual customers.

Once you decide on a florist, be sure to get a written contract stipulating costs, times, dates, places, and services. Make sure the florist is set to arrive before the photographer, so everything will be ready when picture time comes.

Working with Your Florist

Before sitting down to meet with your florist, you should determine what your flower budget is. Flowers are one of the areas of your wedding where there is the potential to spend a huge chunk of change almost without trying. You don't have to go broke buying flowers, however. If you're careful (and maybe a little crafty) you can bring your flowers in under budget—without sacrificing any of the beauty or romance.

An honest florist, when presented with a definite budget figure, will steer you in the most practical direction. Good florists know there's nothing to be gained in making you miserable by showing you things they know you can't afford. But if you don't have (or don't give them) a hint of your budget, many will be quite prepared to tempt you with the most elaborate arrangements.

You'll also need to decide on the color scheme of your wedding before you can begin choosing flowers. Take color swatches along so the florist can recommend flowers that will either match or complement the overall color scheme.

Your florist can also guide you to the flowers that most suit your style and taste. If you're a petite woman, for instance, the florist will probably advise against carrying a large floral arrangement. He or she will also tell you which flowers will go best in the ceremony and reception locations you've chosen. If the florist has never done work at either site before, coordinate a trip so you can both look around and get the feel of things.

The Language of Flowers

With all the hoopla about a certain flower's appearance, you may have forgotten to consider its meaning:

- 🌸 Amaryllis: splendid beauty
- 🌸 Apple blossom: temptation
- 🌸 Bachelor's button: celibacy or hope (depending on who you talk to)
- 🌸 Bluebell: constancy
- 🌸 Buttercup: riches

- Camellia: perfect loveliness, gratitude
- Carnation: pure, deep love
- Daffodil: regard
- Daisy: share your feelings
- Forget-me-not: don't forget (or true love)
- Gardenia: joy
- Honeysuckle: generous and devoted affection, genuine affection
- Ivy: fidelity
- Jasmine: amiability (or grace and elegance)
- Jonquil: affection returned
- Lily: purity
- Lily of the valley: happiness
- Lime: conjugal bliss
- Marigold: sacred affection
- Myrtle: love
- Orange blossom: purity, loveliness
- Red chrysanthemum: I love you
- Red rose: I love you
- Red tulip: love declared
- Rose: love
- Violet: modesty (or faithfulness)
- White camellia: perfect loveliness
- White daisy: innocence
- White lilac: the first emotions of love
- White lily: purity and innocence
- Wood sorrel: joy

Silk Flowers

If you want more in the floral department than you can afford, don't overlook the option of silk. When done well, silk flower arrangements can be as lovely as the real thing. With silk, you also get a broader choice of colors. And while real flowers die quickly, leaving you to lament money you spent on something that didn't last, silk flowers can be kept as decorations or keepsakes long after the wedding.

If you can't bear the thought of not being able to smell the wedding flowers, but also like the advantages of silk, compromise: use live where it's most important to you and silk in other areas. Some brides even have two bouquets made, one real and one silk. They keep whichever they prefer, and use the other one for the infamous bouquet toss.

Flowers for the Bride

In addition to incorporating your favorite flowers, your bridal bouquet should complement your wedding gown and be consistent with the style and level of formality of your wedding. A good florist can point you in the right direction. If you're having a simple wedding in a field or meadow, for instance, the florist may suggest a loose arrangement of wild flowers. On the other hand, if your wedding is very formal with hundreds of guests, an elaborate cascade bouquet might be in order.

If you want to observe the tradition of tossing your bouquet but still keep the one you walked down the aisle with, consider ordering a "tossing bouquet." This is typically a small, simple bouquet. Another option is to have your florist add a detachable, smaller bunch to your bridal bouquet. When the time comes to toss the bouquet, you simply pull out the smaller arrangement.

Flowers for the Wedding Party

Along with that bouquet you'll be tossing, you'll have to choose arrangements for your wedding attendants, the mother of the bride, and the mother of the groom, as well as boutonnieres for the male attendants, the father of the bride, and the father of the groom.

In most weddings, the bridesmaids carry their flowers rather than wear them. These arrangements can range from elaborate bouquets to simple groupings—or even single long-stemmed roses or lilies. (You may decide to add something special to the maid of honor's flowers as a way to make her stand out more.) Floral headpieces can be a lovely touch for your bridesmaids, and also as part of your veil. If you're having a flower girl, she'll need a basket of flower petals or a small bouquet.

The mothers of the marrying couple usually receive special corsages just before the ceremony begins. However, if your ceremony includes any readings about the importance of family (or any similar elements), you may decide to incorporate the act of passing along these flowers as part of the wedding itself. Grandmothers, great-grandmothers, or godmothers attending the ceremony would also appreciate being recognized with a gift of flowers.

Flowers for the men are pretty simple. The ushers wear boutonnieres, usually a carnation or a rose. Sometimes the boutonniere is dyed to match the bridesmaid's dresses; sometimes it's white. The groom wears a lapel spray to match the bride's bouquet, or a traditional boutonniere. The fathers usually have boutonnieres similar to those worn by the ushers. The same goes for grandfathers, great-grandfathers, godfathers, and other special folks.

Flowers for the Ceremony

Flowers are an important part of the ceremony because they accent key points and lend atmosphere. If you're being married in a grand cathedral, the odds are that you'll need a few large, elaborate arrangements to accompany the surroundings; small displays would simply be swallowed up. Likewise, small accent displays would be a perfect complement to a quaint country church; large arrangements would overpower the place.

How much of the ceremony site do you want to decorate with flowers? Some couples simply have one large or a few small arrangements placed around the altar. Others also place flowers on the pews, the windows, and the doors.

Many couples use their ceremony flowers at the reception as well. By using the same flowers, you save yourself the expense of having to decorate both locations. You might even have money left over! All you need to accomplish this feat is a responsible friend or relative to transport the flowers from the ceremony to the reception.

While guests are milling around outside of the ceremony and traveling to the reception site, this trustworthy person will be unloading floral displays. By the time everyone arrives, everything should be all set for the photographer and the guests.

Flowers for the Reception

The flowers at the reception are meant to highlight the overall design scheme. Centerpieces for the guest tables will make the most impact, adding color and beauty. Vases of cut flowers, arrangements in pots or baskets, elegant topiaries, and floral wreaths surrounding hurricane lamps are just a few of the options available to you. Consult with your florist to find the perfect centerpieces for your budget.

The head table should receive a great deal of attention in the flower department, as this will be the focal point of your reception—at least until the dancing begins. In addition to flowers, consider using votif candles and garlands of greenery to dress up the head table.

You should also place flowers or decorations atop the buffet or wedding cake tables; you'll give people something to look at while they think about food. Flowers can also be used to decorate the wedding cake itself. And depending on the atmosphere of your reception site, potted plants, hanging plants, and small trees can add a festive air to the proceedings.

Preserving Your Bouquet

Many brides choose to preserve their bridal bouquet as a memento of the wedding. In reality, the odds are very strong that your bouquet will end up in storage (which often means "someplace no one remembers"). Keep this in mind if you decide to take your bouquet to the florist for preservation; the process will probably cost you more than the bouquet itself. There are, however, cheaper and more practical ways for you to preserve your bouquet yourself. If you do decide to take advantage of them, you can spend the money on something else, like your honeymoon.

PRESSING

Pressing is the most popular method of bouquet preservation. Your first step is to take a picture of the bouquet; you'll need it to refer to later. Take the bouquet apart (yes, apart) and place the separate flowers in the pages of heavy books, between sheets of blank white paper. (If not cushioned by blank paper, ink from the book's pages will ruin the flowers.) The flowers should be kept in the books for two to six weeks, depending on their size. (The bigger the flower, the more time it will need.) When the flowers look ready, glue them onto a mounting board in an arrangement that closely resembles the original bouquet in the photo. Place the board in a picture frame and hang it wherever you desire. (This process works best when it's started soon after your wedding, because the flowers have had less time to wilt.)

HANGING/DRYING

Again, snap a photo for reference and take the bouquet apart. To preserve their shape and prevent drooping, hang the flowers upside down to dry. Some color may be lost in the drying process (the loss is less if the flowers are hung in a dark room). When the flowers are completely dry, spray them with shellac or silica gel for protection. Then reassemble them to match the photo. As with pressing, the earlier you start the process, the more successful it's likely to be.

POTPOURRI

For this method, you'll need to buy some netting or lacy fabric. Dry the flowers and gather the petals together. Place small piles of the petals into four-inch squares of the netting, then tie the squares into little pouches with ribbon. These little sachets can be placed anywhere, filling the air with a little reminder of your wedding day.

Florist Worksheet

Name of florist:

Address:

Telephone: Contact:

Hours:

Directions:

Appointments:

Date: Time:

Date: Time:

Date: Time:

Services provided:

Date of delivery: Time:

Location of bridal party:

Travel fee:

Additional fees (if any):

Cost:

Total amount due:

Amount of deposit: Date:

Balance due: Date:

Sales tax included?   ❏ Yes   ❏ No

Terms of cancellation:

Notes:

Person/Item	Description	Number	Cost
BRIDE			
Bouquet			
Headpiece			
Toss-away bouquet			
Going-away corsage			
MAID/MATRON OF HONOR			
Bouquet			
Headpiece			
BRIDESMAIDS			
Bouquet			
Headpiece			
FLOWER GIRLS			
Flowers			
Basket			
Headpiece			
MOTHERS OF THE BRIDE AND GROOM			
Corsage			
GRANDMOTHERS OF THE BRIDE AND GROOM			
Corsage			
GROOM			
Boutonniere			
BEST MAN			
Boutonniere			
USHERS			
Boutonniere			
RINGBEARER			
Boutonniere			
Pillow			
FATHERS OF THE BRIDE AND GROOM			
Boutonniere			
GRANDFATHERS OF THE BRIDE AND GROOM			
Boutonniere			
READERS			
Corsage			
Boutonniere			
OTHER (LIST BELOW)			
TOTAL			

Item	Description	Number	Cost
Aisle runner			
Altar flowers			
Garland			
Potted flowers			
Potted plants			
Pews/chair flowers			
Pews/chair bows			
Candelabra			
Candle holders			
Candles			
Unity candle			
Wedding arch			
Columns			
Trellis			
Wreaths for church doors			
Other (list below)			
TOTAL			

Item	Description	Number	Cost
GUEST TABLES			
Centerpieces			
Garland			
Candles			
HEAD TABLE			
Centerpieces			
Garland			
Candles			
BUFFET TABLE			
Flowers			
Garland			
Decorations			
CAKE TABLE			
Cake top			
Flowers			
Garland			
Decorations			
GUEST BOOK TABLE			
Flowers			
Decorations			
ENVELOPE TABLE			
Flowers			
Decorations			
CANDELABRA			
CANDLE HOLDERS			
CANDLES			
ARCHWAY			
COLUMNS			
TRELLIS			
WREATHS			
GARLANDS			
POTTED FLOWERS			
POTTED PLANTS			
HANGING PLANTS			
OTHER (LIST BELOW)			
TOTAL			

CHAPTER FIFTEEN

WEDDING INVITATIONS AND STATIONERY

After the guest list is finished and your fiancé has succeeded in changing your mind about wanting to elope, you will probably start thinking about wedding invitations. As you pore through book after book of possible choices, keep in mind that the style of wedding invitation you ultimately choose will be the first indication most guests receive as to the type of wedding you'll be having. Needless to say, the invitations and printing process you ultimately choose should be consistent with your wedding style and level of formality.

Selecting a Stationer

The way most brides find invitations these days is by going to a stationery store and browsing through the invitation catalogs. These catalogs contain samples in which the paper stock, borders, and any ornamentation have already been set. You pick out the color of the paper and ink, the style of the script, and the words to use. Some invitations also come complete with phrasing; all you do is supply the information for your wedding and the manufacturer does the rest.

These sample catalogs are created by a handful of large printers who currently dominate the invitation market. By printing several lines of mass-produced invitations, these companies are able to offer a greater variety and a cheaper price than a private printer. Because these companies are the main source of wedding invitations, you'll probably see the same sample catalogs in the majority of places you look.

You may have heard about personal stationers or printers, those people who will design a unique invitation for you, and then print it. However, because of the ease and popularity of the catalog method, doing invitations this way is becoming a thing of the past. Private stationers and printers simply can't afford the overhead costs of offering the broad selection that large manufacturers do.

If you can't find a catalog invitation that you like, or if you want something too specific to be found in a catalog, you may need to go the route of the private printer. Check the business section of your phone directory under "Printers."

Printing Methods

There are various methods of printing invitations. They can vary greatly in terms of cost, and generally speaking, you get what you pay for. Ask to see samples produced by the various methods available, and choose what you like and what fits in your budget. Here are the five main methods.

ENGRAVING

Engraving is the most elegant form of putting ink on paper. The paper is "stamped" from the back by metal plates the printer creates that raise the letters up off of the paper as they're printed. Unfortunately, you'll be asked to pay extra for all that elegance, so unless you have a very big invitation budget, engraving may not be for you. You will almost certainly have to sign on with a smaller printer (rather than one of the big national operations) if you want to go this route.

THERMOGRAPHY

Right now, the most popular way to put the ink on your invitations is called "thermography." By using a special press that heats the ink, the printer creates a raised-letter effect that is almost indistinguishable from engraving. What is distinguishable, however, is the price, which is about half the cost of engraving. (Most mass-produced invitations are done by thermography these days.)

OFFSET PRINTING

Offset printing, also known as flat printing, is the most common form of printing. If you choose to do your invitations this way, you may have to find a small private printer, since most of the big catalog manufacturers are only set up for thermography. While some may consider the offset method boring or unappealing (the letters aren't raised at all), it's the only form of printing that allows you to work with multiple ink colors.

CALLIGRAPHY

Calligraphy (that fancy formal script) is an up-and-coming approach in the invitation world. If you've always admired the style of calligraphy, but didn't think you could afford to have a calligrapher letter your invitations by hand, recent developments may make you reconsider. Some printers are now able to reproduce the look of calligraphy by using a computerized font—a method that is considerably faster (and cheaper) than the human hand. Any sadness you may feel over the computerization of yet another art form is likely to be tempered by your sudden ability to afford it. If you are interested in hiring a true calligrapher, ask your local stationery store for referrals or check the Yellow Pages.

HANDWRITTEN INVITATIONS

If you're inviting fifty people or fewer, the etiquette gods will allow you to write your invitations out by hand. That may not be good news for your hand, which will probably start cramping after invitation number ten, but it's very good news for your pocketbook. Obviously, this is not a job for someone with messy handwriting. If yours is suspect, recruit the groom, your mother, or anyone else who's up for the job and can do it well.

Wording Your Invitations

The bride's family traditionally sponsors the wedding, and is therefore listed on the invitation, but if you and your fiancé desire, you can name stepparents or his family on the invitation as well.

Below are several examples of formally worded invitations that should fit most situations. Keep in mind that circumstances can vary greatly when dealing with difficult family issues like divorce, so use the examples as a general guideline. The same holds true with religious wording; it's best to check with the officiant before printing the invitations, as the wording will vary with affiliations.

It is important to note that a deceased parent's name should never appear on a wedding invitation. If one of your parents has passed away, you should try to find some other way to honor his or her memory during the ceremony and reception.

TRADITIONAL WORDING

Mr. and Mrs. Joseph Moran
request the honor of your presence
at the marriage of their daughter
Margaret Ann
to
Mr. Justin McCann
on Saturday, the third of July
at three o'clock
Holy Trinity Lutheran Church
Chicago, Illinois

GROOM'S PARENTS SPONSOR

Mr. and Mrs. Anthony Russo
request the honor of your presence
at the marriage of
Miss Christina Lynn Marconi
to their son
Mr. Paul Dominic Russo

BRIDE AND GROOM'S PARENTS COSPONSOR

Mr. and Mrs. David Silverman
and
Mr. and Mrs. Leonard Berkowitz
request the honor of your presence
at the marriage of their children
Miss Sharon Ruth Silverman
and
Mr. Mark Abraham Berkowitz

BRIDE AND GROOM SPONSOR

*The honor of your presence is requested
at the marriage of
Miss Cynthia Cho
and
Mr. Joseph Wong*
or
*Miss Cynthia Cho
and
Mr. Joseph Wong
request the honor of your presence
at their marriage*

BRIDE'S MOTHER, NOT REMARRIED, SPONSORS

*Mrs. Patricia Rodriquez
requests the honor of your presence
at the marriage of her daughter
Diana Elizabeth*

BRIDE'S MOTHER, REMARRIED, SPONSORS

*Mrs. Patricia Clark
requests the honor of your presence
at the marriage of her daughter
Diana Elizabeth Rodriquez*

BRIDE'S MOTHER AND STEPFATHER SPONSOR

*Mr. and Mrs. Michael Wlodarczyk
requests the honor of your presence
at the marriage of her daughter
Rebecca Mullen*

BRIDE'S FATHER, REMARRIED OR NOT, SPONSORS

Mr. Kevin O'Neill
requests the honor of your presence
at the marriage of his daughter
Kerri Ann

BRIDE'S FATHER AND STEPMOTHER SPONSOR

Mr. and Mrs. Nasir Chopra
request the honor of your presence
at the marriage of his daughter
Chandra

BRIDE'S DIVORCED PARENTS, NOT REMARRIED, CO-SPONSOR

Mrs. Laura Smith Dubois
and
Mr. Charles Dubois
request the honor of your presence
at the marriage of their daughter
Denise Marie

BRIDE'S DIVORCED PARENTS, REMARRIED, CO-SPONSOR

Mrs. Michael Kyriakos
and
Mr. Nikos Diamandis
request the honor of your presence
at the marriage of their daughter
Susan Fotini

PROTESTANT WORDING

Mr. and Mrs. Joseph Moran
are pleased to invite you
to join in a Christian celebration
of the marriage of their daughter
Margaret Ann

CATHOLIC WORDING

Mr. and Mrs. Vincent Magnani
request the honor of your presence
at the Nuptial Mass
at which their daughter
Angela Marcella
and
Thomas Patrick Flaherty
will be united in the
Sacrament of Holy Matrimony

JEWISH WORDING

Mr. and Mrs. Jeremy Greene
and
Mr. and Mrs. Michael Cohen
request the honor of your presence
at the marriage of their children
Susan Paige
to
William Samuel

Reception and Response Cards

Along with the wedding invitation, most people include a separate reception
card, which lists where and when the reception will be held. Also included

is a response card, which indicates whether or not the invitee will be able to attend, and if he or she is bringing a guest. Response cards come with a return envelope, which is already stamped and addressed to the wedding sponsors in order to facilitate the RSVP process.

Following is a sample wording of reception and response cards.

RECEPTION CARD

> *Reception*
> *immediately following the ceremony*
> *Windy Hill Country Club*
> *60 Canterbury Road*
> *Chicago, Illinois*

RESPONSE CARD

> *The favor of your reply is requested*
> *by the first of June*
> *M* _____
> *Number of persons* _____

Additional Stationery

Aside from the wedding invitation, there are other specialty items available. Thank-you notes are an absolute must, but whether or not you choose to use these other products depends on the level of formality of your wedding, your preference, and your budget.

CEREMONY CARDS

Ceremony cards (guaranteeing entrance into the proceedings) are not necessary for a traditional wedding site, but if your wedding is being held at a public place (such as a museum or a historic mansion), you may want to have some way to distinguish your guests from the tourists.

PEW CARDS

You will need pew cards if you wish to reserve seats at the ceremony for any special family and friends. Obviously, you'll want to have them sit as close to where the action will occur as possible. If you send these special guests pew cards, they can give them to the usher at the ceremony; he will then know to seat them in the front sections you will have marked off as "Reserved."

RAIN CARDS

If you're having your ceremony and/or reception outdoors, you should use rain cards to notify people of an alternate location in the event of rain.

TRAVEL CARDS/MAPS

You should include directions to the ceremony and reception sites in any invitations you send to out-of-town guests. Any maps you send will add to the usefulness of the directions, provided that they are well drawn.

WEDDING ANNOUNCEMENTS

Announcements are usually sent out after the wedding to business associates, faraway family and friends, and others who were not present at the wedding. The announcement simply passes on word of your nuptials, but it does not obligate the receiver to send a wedding gift.

AT-HOME CARDS

These cards let people know your new name, your new address, and when you'll be moved in. You can also use at-home cards to let people know whether you have taken your husband's name and how you prefer to be addressed. To add to your paper trail, there is an entirely different kind of card dedicated solely to the name issue, known as a name card. If you wish, you can send your address information on the at-home card, and your name preference on the name card, but it really is more sensible—and affordable—to combine the information onto one.

THANK-YOU NOTES

Thank-you notes are sometimes referred to as informals. You can order thank-you notes that match your invitations, or you can choose something completely different. Despite the name, the notes can be as formal or informal as you like. If you already have personal stationery, you might consider using that for your thank-you notes instead of ordering something new. It's perfectly proper as far as etiquette is concerned, and you might save some money.

CEREMONY PROGRAMS

Ceremony programs are to a wedding what a playbill is to a concert or play. The program identifies the order of the ceremony, the participants, the music, and the readings. Ceremony programs can be an elegant touch, especially if they're professionally designed and printed. If you don't have a great deal of extra money, but you do have a friend with very nice penmanship, artistic talent, or a good personal computer system, you can create the program yourself and photocopy enough sheets for all of your guests.

PARTY FAVORS AND MORE

You can also get napkins, matchbooks, pens, pencils, and almost anything else under the sun with your name and wedding date printed on it. Just remember, though, that you could be spending the money on your honeymoon.

Ordering Your Wedding Stationery

Your wedding stationery should be ordered after you've determined the date, times, and locations of the ceremony and reception, but not before the guest list is finalized—about three months prior to the wedding. Invitations should be mailed about eight weeks before the big day. If your wedding falls near a holiday, mail out your invitations a few weeks earlier to give your guests some extra time to plan. (Of course, this means you'll probably have to order your invitations earlier, too.) This should give you plenty of time to give a final head count to the caterer. Also, as regrets come in, you can send invitations to those people squeezed off the original guest list.

Since you'll be addressing the invitations by hand, you'll probably want to order some extras in case you make a mistake. Also, if you have any "standby" guests, you'll need the extras to send out. In any case, you will probably like to have a few invitations as keepsakes.

Be sure to proofread everything before you place the final order. There's nothing quite like receiving a box of three hundred invitations on which your name is spelled wrong—and the year of your wedding is given as "1492."

If you're pressed for time, ask your printer to provide you with the envelopes in advance. That way, you can write them out while the invitations are being printed. Most mass-produced invitation orders are turned around within three to four weeks, so unless you're under some pretty remarkable scheduling pressure, you should have plenty of time.

Addressing and Assembling the Invitations

It's a good idea to enlist the help of a few family members or friends with good penmanship to address and assemble your invitations. But don't recruit so many people that things become confusing. Make sure the same person who writes the information on the inside of an invitation also addresses its outer envelope. This makes the invitation package look uniform, and lets the person receiving it know that it was put together with care.

You will need:

- Your wedding stationery
- Several friends and/or family members with good penmanship
- Several pens (use black ink only)
- Stamps for the invitations and response cards (ask for the self-adhesive kind to make your job easier)
- Envelope moisteners (unless you want to lick all those envelopes!)

By now you should have found out how much postage you will need to mail your invitations. Sometimes, with heavy paper and lots of inserts, the whole package requires more than a standard first-class stamp. The return envelope needs only a standard first-class stamp, which you are also expected to provide.

Before you begin, you should be aware of the two big invitation-writing taboos. Taboo number one is using a typewriter or printed label to address an invitation envelope. Invitations should always be addressed by hand. Taboo number two is using abbreviations. Exceptions are generally made only for Mr., Mrs., and Ms. And although the etiquette police might holler, the post office and your weary helpers will thank you for using abbreviated state names.

When addressing the outer envelope, include the full name of the person or persons you are inviting; on the inner envelope, you can be more casual.

OUTER ENVELOPE
Mr. and Mrs. Stephen Michael McGill
(or Ms. Linda Ann Smith and Mr. Stephen Michael McGill)
16 Maple Drive
Chestnut Hill, Massachusetts 02555

INNER ENVELOPE
Mr. and Mrs. McGill
(or Stephen and Linda)

If you are inviting the whole family, the approach is pretty much the same.

OUTER ENVELOPE
Mr. and Mrs. Stephen Michael McGill and Family
(or The McGill Family)
16 Maple Drive
Chestnut Hill, Massachusetts 02555

INNER ENVELOPE
Mr. and Mrs. McGill
Andrea, Paul, and Meg

When you are inviting a single person with a guest, the outer envelope should be addressed to him or her only; the inner envelope includes the phrase "and guest."

Now that you've got everything addressed and ready to go, what's the best way to assemble the invitations? Unless your stationer supplied assembly instructions along with your invitations, packing up the invitation and its extras can be as frustrating and complicated as making out your seating plan. Here's a method that should make things easier for you:

1. Stamp the response card envelope.
2. Place the response card face-up under the flap of the response card envelope.
3. Place a piece of tissue paper over the lettering on the invitation (optional).
4. Place the response card and envelope, along with all other insertions inside the invitation, face-side up.
5. Insert the invitation face-side up in the inner envelope. Do not seal it.
6. Insert the inner envelope into the outer envelope so that the handwritten names face the back of the outer envelope.
7. Seal the outer envelope. Make sure the envelope is properly addressed and contains your return address.
8. Stamp and mail the invitation, using the correct postage.

Name of stationer: _____

Address: _____

Telephone: _____ Contact: _____

Hours: _____

Directions: _____

Appointments:

Date: _____ Time: _____

Date: _____ Time: _____

Date: _____ Time: _____

Wedding invitations:

Description: _____

Manufacturer: _____

Style: _____

Paper: _____

Paper color: _____

Typeface: _____

Ink color: _____

Printing process: _____

Tissue paper inserts: _____

Printed outer envelopes: _____

Inner envelopes: _____

Envelope liner: _____

Number ordered: _____

Cost: _____

Reception Cards:

Description: _____

Number ordered: _____

Cost: _____

Response Cards:

Description: _____

Printed envelopes: _____

Envelope liner: _____

Number ordered: _____

Cost: _____

Ceremony Cards:

Description: _____

Number ordered: _____

Cost: _____

Pew Cards:

Description: _____

Number ordered: _____

Cost: _____

Rain Cards:

Description: _____

Number ordered: _____

Cost: _____

Travel Cards/Maps:

Description:

Number ordered:

Cost:

Wedding Announcements:

Description:

Printed envelopes:

Envelope liner:

Number ordered:

Cost:

At-home Cards:

Description:

Printed envelopes:

Envelope liner:

Number ordered:

Cost:

Thank-you Notes:

Description:

Printed envelopes:

Envelope liner:

Number ordered:

Cost:

Ceremony Programs:

Description:

Number ordered:

Cost:

Party Favors:

Description:

Number ordered:

Cost:

Other:

Description:

Number ordered:

Cost:

Order date:

Ready date: Time:

Delivery/Pick-up instructions:

Cost:

Total amount due:

Amount of deposit: Date:

Balance due: Date:

Sales tax included?   ❑ Yes   ❑ No

Terms of cancellation:

Notes:

Wedding invitations:

Return address for invitation envelopes:

Reception cards:

Response cards:

Return address for response card envelopes:

Ceremony cards:

Pew cards:

Rain cards:

Travel cards:

At-home cards: _____

_____

_____

_____

Return address for at-home card envelopes: _____

Thank-you notes: _____

Return address for thank-you note envelopes: _____

Ceremony programs: _____

_____

_____

_____

_____

_____

Party favors: _____

Other: _____

_____

_____

_____

Notes: _____

_____

_____

CHAPTER SIXTEEN

YOUR WEDDING CAKE

The wedding cake originated in medieval times as a symbol of fertility. But before you decide to abandon the whole wedding cake idea, rest assured that for the most part, the cake has since lost most of its symbolism and now functions more as an edible work of art. And thanks to innovative bakers and cake designers, you can have the cake of your dreams and eat it too!

Choosing a Baker

Begin your search for the right bakery at least three months before the wedding. Wedding cakes sometimes require so much time and detail that bakers will work on no more than one per week.

The baker should provide you with sample books to help you pick out your cake design; once you've found one you like, you can move on to questions of size, flavors, fillings, and frostings. If you'd like the colors on the cake to match your wedding colors, bring a sample swatch to the baker. Most important, you should be sure to taste samples of any cake you commission. Your cake could be lovely to look at, but that won't count for much if two hundred people can't quite manage to swallow it.

Flavors and Decorations

Once upon a time, a wedding cake was white inside and out, but today there are countless options for flavors and decorations. Consider these cakes: German chocolate, chocolate fudge, devil's food, carrot spice, lemon zest, mocha, banana sour cream, orange poppy seed, Kahlua, Amaretto, Irish cream, and even cheesecake. And there's no need to stop there: add fillings to your cake or serve it with something on the side, such as a sauce, fresh whipped cream, fresh fruits, flavored custards, or mousse. As for frostings, you might consider different flavors of buttercreams, cream cheese frosting, chocolate ganache, fondant (a smooth icing made of powdered sugar and corn syrup), or even marzipan!

Your cake may be garnished with fresh or confection flowers, greenery, and decorations such as columns. The icing or frosting can be made to match the wedding colors you've selected.

If money is no object, consider having a cake specifically designed for you and your fiancé—one that perhaps reflects your hobbies or honeymoon destination. Or consider a cake shaped like a castle, a gazebo, or a basket of flowers. Be creative, and you can turn your wedding cake into a genuine work of art.

Cost

Most people are prepared for the expense of the caterer, the band, the photographer, and so on, but few realize just how much dough (no pun intended) is needed for even a modest wedding cake. Wedding cake prices are usually based on a per-person basis, plus extra charges for special flavors, icings, and decorations. A typical cake may cost from $2 to $4 per person; add to that $2 to $3 per person if you simply must have that stylish fondant frosting. Colors, decorations, tiers, and fancy extras also add to the cost. Do the math and your head might start to whirl!

Rest assured, there *are* ways to cut costs. Remember, your decorated cake does not have to serve all the guests. Save money by ordering a smaller decorated cake, along with a supplemental sheet cake to feed your guests. On the other hand, if dessert is already included on your wedding menu, there's really no need for a wedding cake except for the traditional cake-cutting ceremony. If that's the case, you can cut costs by making it as small and simple as possible.

How to Cut the Wedding Cake

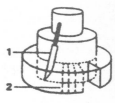

Cut vertically through the bottom layer to the edge of the second layer (1). Then cut wedge-shaped pieces as shown by (2).

When these pieces have been served, do the same with the middle layer. Cut vertically around at the edge of the top layer (3), then cut pieces as shown by (4).

When those pieces have been served, return to the botom layer and repeat the cuts (5) and (6).

The remaining tiers may be cut into desired size pieces.

Preserving the Top Layer of Your Cake

Traditionally, the bride and groom preserve the top tier of their wedding cake so that they can eat it on their first anniversary. To freeze the cake, wrap it tightly in plastic, place it in a sturdy box, and wrap it in plastic again. Thaw for approximately twelve hours in the wrappings and enjoy!

The Groom's Cake

The groom's cake is usually a fruitcake or other dark cake, such as chocolate, which is cut and put into boxes as a favor for guests. Many grooms have a cake made in the shape of a favorite hobby, such as a football. Groom's cakes are very common in the South, but their popularity is growing in other regions as well. As legend has it, single guests who sleep with a piece of the groom's cake under their pillow will dream of their future husband or wife.

Baker Worksheet

Name of bakery:

Address:

Telephone:

Contact:

Hours:

Directions:

Appointments:

Date: Time:

Date: Time:

Date: Time:

Order date:

Delivery/Pick-up date: Time:

Delivery/Pick-up instructions:

Cost:

Total amount due:

Amount of deposit: Date:

Balance due: Date:

Sales tax included?   ❑ Yes   ❑ No

Terms of cancellation:

Notes:

Item	Description	Cost
WEDDING CAKE		
Size		
Shape		
Number of tiers		
Number cake will serve		
Flavor of cake		
Flavor of filling		
Flavor of icing		
Icing decorations		
Cake top		
Cake decorations		
Other		
GROOM'S CAKE		
Size		
Shape		
Number cake will serve		
Flavor		
Icing		
Cake top		
Cake decorations		
Other		
CAKE SERVING SET		
CAKE BOXES		
DELIVERY CHARGE		
OTHER (LIST BELOW)		
TOTAL		

CHAPTER SEVENTEEN

WEDDING TRANSPORTATION

Picture yourself making the perfect entrance at your wedding ceremony. Are you trotting to the church door via a romantic horse-drawn carriage, pulling up in a sleek limousine, or arriving in a convertible antique car with your veil in the wind? These days, there are more options than ever as far as wedding transportation goes. In fact, innovative couples have been known to use helicopters, boats, street trolleys, hot-air balloons, motor cycles, and even parade floats!

Keep in mind that above all, your wedding transportation must be reliable. After all, you'll want to make sure that you, your fiancé, and your wedding party all arrive at the ceremony safely and on time. It's also important to make sure everyone knows what car is taking whom where. You and your groom, for instance, should make sure you have some way to get to the hotel or the airport after the reception. If you don't have a hired car to do the job, arrange for a friend to drive your going-away car to the reception site, so you can drive yourselves.

Limousines

Limousines are by far the most common mode of wedding transportation. Let's face it, they're what first comes to mind when you think about luxury transportation. Though it may not be as original or exciting as arriving in, say, a Blue Angels fighter plane, showing up in a well-kept limousine is certainly nothing to scoff at. In what other car can you seat ten people comfortably (not that you'd want that many with you on your wedding day), watch TV, serve yourself from the bar, and have a chauffeur at your beck and call?—certainly not the family station wagon. And a big shiny limousine is still impressive enough to instill awe in the occupants of those boring regular cars who are sitting next to it in traffic.

Most couples hire one limousine. Usually, this necessitates a number of passenger exchanges on the wedding day. Here's how it works. The bride gets the first ride in the limo; it transports her, her father, and sometimes the bride's attendants to the ceremony site. (How the groom makes it to the site is, of course, his problem.) After the ceremony, the bride swaps guys and returns to the limousine with her groom, and the two of them ride to the reception, perhaps with their wedding party. Depending upon the length of the limousine rental, the newlyweds might also be driven in style to their hotel after the reception, or perhaps to the airport to begin their honeymoon.

If your budget has room, you may choose to rent one or two additional limousines to transport attendants and parents. This not only saves you the hassle of coordinating other transportation for them, but it will also leave them thinking you're really swell.

Hiring a Reliable Limousine Service

A recently married friend or relative may be able to recommend a reliable limousine service with good cars—and thereby save you a lot of legwork. But if you're not that lucky, put on your Educated Consumer hat and get out there, look at the cars, and ask some questions.

Try to find a company that owns its limousines. Owners are more likely to keep track of a car's maintenance (and whereabouts)—many limos have seen their share of unauthorized excursions. Some limo services rent cars out from another company, which means those cars are probably being shared by several other services. In addition to the maintenance and overuse problems, it's harder for a company that doesn't own its own limos to ensure the availability of any given car, or to supply you with a car of the color and size that you want.

Make sure you verify a service's license and insurance coverage. Get references; verify that its chauffeurs show up on time, are courteous, don't break the speed limit, and don't have a habit of driving into trees.

Inspect all of the cars. Are they good-looking inside and out? Are they what you want? Don't take a company's word that it can supply a white stretch limo with a burgundy interior. Get a look at it yourself before you commit to anything.

Most limousine services charge by the hour. Unfortunately for you, the clock starts the second the driver leaves the base, not the moment he or she starts driving you around. (If you can find a service that's based near your home and the festivities, you'll be saving yourself a little money.)

Find out exact costs—and what you'll be getting for your money. Does the limo company provide champagne? Ice? Glasses? Can you save a lot of money by bringing these items yourself? Is there an extra charge for a TV and a bar?

Once you decide on a limousine service, get all the details finalized in a written contract. It should specify the type of car, any additional options and services you will need, the expected length of service, the date, and the time. It's a good idea to arrange for the limo to arrive at least fifteen to thirty minutes before you're going to need it, just to be on the safe side.

The chauffeur's tip is generally 10 to 20 percent of the total bill, and is usually included in the flat fee. But don't take that for granted; check to make sure. You don't want to "stiff" someone who has provided you with good service and helped make your day run (or ride) smoothly. By the same token, if you are dissatisfied with the service your chauffeur provides, speak up—and don't be afraid to ask for your money back.

Other Stylish Rides

If you want something less conventional, but don't like the idea of flying, boating, or taking the subway, there are plenty of luxury and antique cars out there available for rental. Are you the white Rolls type? Perhaps a silver Bentley would suit you best. If you've got some extra cash on hand, go all out—snag an Excalibur. It will make for a truly unforgettable shot in your wedding video.

If your budget prevents you from renting wedding transportation, look around for family and friends who may have large luxury cars that they'd be willing to lend you. Some car buffs are likely to be horrified at the idea of someone else behind the wheel of their baby; reassure them that if they wish, they are more than welcome to play the part of chauffeur for the day. The only requirement here is that the cars be clean (you're responsible for the cost of their prewedding car wash). And be sure to remember your generous donors with a little gift and a full tank of gas.

Name of company:

Address:

Telephone:

Contact: Hours:

Directions:

Services provided:

Number of vehicles rented:

Description:

Cost per hour:

Minimum number of hours:

Overtime cost:

Hours of rental:

Name of driver(s):

Cost:

Total amount due:

Amount of deposit: Date:

Balance due: Date:

Sales tax included?   ❏ Yes   ❏ No

Terms of cancellation:

Notes:

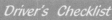

Give a copy of this to each driver.

Vehicle:

Driver:

Date:

Name of bride and groom:

1. Place of pick-up: Arrival time:

Names of passenger(s):

Address:

Telephone:

Directions:

Special instructions:

2. Place of pick-up: Arrival time:

Names of passenger(s):

Address:

Telephone:

Directions:

Special instructions:

3. Place of pick-up: _____ Arrival time: _____

Names of passenger(s): _____

Address: _____

_____

Telephone: _____

Directions: _____

_____

Special instructions: _____

4. Ceremony location: _____ Arrival time: _____

Names of passenger(s): _____

Address: _____

_____

Telephone: _____

Directions: _____

_____

Special instructions: _____

5. Reception location: _____ Arrival time: _____

Names of passenger(s): _____

Address: _____

_____

Telephone: _____

Directions: _____

_____

Special instructions: _____

INTO THE SUNSET

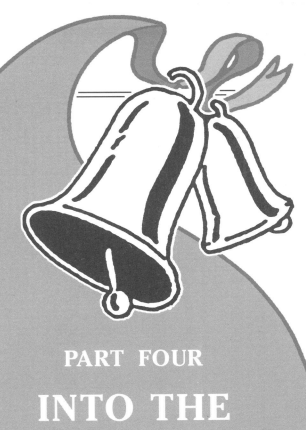

PART FOUR

INTO THE SUNSET

CHAPTER EIGHTEEN

PLANNING YOUR HONEYMOON

By now you've probably discovered that, what with all the frenzied planning, coordinating, organizing, and worrying involved, getting married can be a full-time job—and then some! When it's all over with, you'll need more than just an ordinary vacation to recuperate.

On the surface, a honeymoon is no different from any other vacation you might take. You pack your bags, make your reservations, and leave home for fun in the sun, snow, or wherever. But a honeymoon is much more than that; it's a man and woman's first getaway together as a married couple, and perhaps the ultimate romantic experience. Ten years from now, you probably won't remember just when it was you spent that summer week in the mountains, or that long weekend skiing, but you're bound to remember nearly every detail of your honeymoon.

Once you and your fiancé agree on where you'd like to (and can afford to) spend your honeymoon, you should talk to a travel agent and start making your reservations. Some of the more popular tourist and honeymoon spots can be booked solid up to a year in advance, so call early—especially if you've got your heart set on a particular location.

Honeymoon Ideas

Just in case you don't have a dream destination in mind, here is a list of some of the most popular honeymoon spots:

The Caribbean:
- Aruba
- Cayman Islands
- Little Dix Bay, British Virgin Islands
- Montego Bay, Jamaica
- Nassau, Bahamas
- Negril, Jamaica
- Ocho Rios, Jamaica
- Paradise Island, Bahamas
- St. Croix

Europe:

- Greece
- Spain
- England
- France
- Italy
- Germany
- Austria
- Switzerland
- Sweden
- Finland
- Norway
- The Netherlands
- Monaco

United States:

- Alaska (an Alaskan cruise)
- Grand Canyon National Park (Arizona)
- The Pacific Coast Highway (California)
- Disneyland (Anaheim, California)
- Walt Disney World (Orlando, Florida)
- The Florida Keys
- Hawaii
- Cape Cod, Martha's Vineyard, and Nantucket (Massachusetts)
- Niagara Falls (New York)
- Hilton Head (South Carolina)
- The Poconos (Pennsylvania)
- Puerto Rico
- U.S. Virgin Islands

Canada:

- Montreal
- Toronto
- Quebec
- Nova Scotia

Mexico:
- The Baja California region
- Cancun
- Guadalajara
- Isla de Cozumel
- Puerto Vallarta

And don't forget about more exotic locations like Tahiti, Fiji, Australia, Japan, Hong Kong, South America, and Africa!

Ultimately, of course, your budget is likely to have at least as big an impact on the destination you choose as your dreams do. But here's a word of advice: don't despair of your desired trip just because you think it's beyond your means. Research all the details. Consult a travel agent on low-priced airfares, reduced-rate package deals, and other ways to save money. You may be pleasantly surprised.

Your First Night

When planning your honeymoon getaway, don't forget to make plans for your first night together. Particularly if you are having an evening reception, you will probably want to rent a room at a hotel or country inn somewhere near your reception location. Tell the hotel manager that you're newlyweds; he or she is likely to send you a bottle of champagne for the occasion. And if your travel plans will accommodate it, plan to spend most of the next morning quietly recovering from the festivities and excitement.

Should You Use a Travel Agent?

Perhaps you're used to handling your vacation arrangements by yourself, without the help of a travel agent. If you're going out of the country, however, you may wish to work with an agent to help you figure out the nuances of international travel. Because foreign vacations can get very complicated—with connecting flights that have to meet boats that have to meet trains—putting all the responsibility in the hands of a trained agent may be a good idea. After all, you've already got enough to do with planning the wedding.

Your agent will tell you what paperwork, identification, and any other necessities you will need in order to travel abroad. With the exception of Canada, Mexico, and some parts of the Caribbean, you'll need a passport, which takes at least six weeks (and sometimes longer) to obtain. Here are some other documents you may need that may take some time to track down:

- Birth certificate
- Driver's license (or other picture ID)
- Proof of marriage
- Proof of citizenship

Additionally, some more exotic destinations require you to receive inoculations before you leave on your trip. Your travel agent should be able to provide such information to you.

Traveling Tips

You should employ a little basic traveler's savvy on your honeymoon. You will need to give some thought to security and safety, just as you would with any other vacation.

Try to use traveler's checks rather than cash whenever possible. The major brands are accepted in just about every foreign country, and unlike cash, they can be replaced if lost or stolen.

Keep all important items in a carry-on bag; that way, you'll still have them if the rest of your luggage is lost or stolen. What goes in such a bag?

- Tickets
- Emergency cash
- Valuable jewelry (except for your wedding ring, though, it might be prudent to leave this at home)
- Driver's licenses
- Proof of age and citizenship
- Passports, visas (if appropriate)
- Eyewear
- Medication

- 🌺 List of luggage contents (for insurance purposes if luggage is lost or stolen)
- 🌺 List of traveler's check numbers (kept separate from checks)
- 🌺 List of credit card numbers
- 🌺 Name and phone number of someone to contact in case of emergency
- 🌺 Checking account numbers
- 🌺 A change of clothes

If you are traveling to a place with a high incidence of petty crime, you may also wish to bring a money belt or pouch to wear under your clothes. These are handy for carrying cash, passports, and any other hard-to-replace items.

Confirm all of your reservations the week before you leave. There's nothing quite like dragging all your heavy luggage into a hotel lobby in some exotic locale, desiring only a soft bed—to find that you don't even have a room.

Assuming you do get a room, don't be afraid to complain to the management if the service or accommodations are not to your satisfaction. And don't wait until you're about to leave to let people know about any problems. Report problems as soon as possible so the situation can be remedied and you can enjoy yourselves.

Items to Remember

Don't get caught running around the house in your wedding dress, throwing clothes into a suitcase while you wait for the limo to arrive. Not only is this undignified, it's a recipe for trouble. Haste may make waste, but it can also make for forgetfulness.

To avoid such last-minute trouble, you should pack for your trip a few days to a week before the wedding. And in addition to the items listed in the previous section, make sure you've packed the following items:

- 🌺 Camera
- 🌺 Film (and plenty of it)
- 🌺 Batteries (for camera)

- Cosmetics
- Deodorant
- Hair dryer
- Brush or comb
- Corkscrew or bottle opener
- Shampoo
- Conditioner
- Toothbrushes and toothpaste
- Disposable razors (and blades)
- Q-tips
- Nail clippers or scissors
- First-aid kit
- Feminine hygiene products
- Aspirin
- Antacids

For the beach:
- Bathing suits
- Sandals
- Coverups
- Sunscreen
- Sunglasses
- Beach bag

For the snow:
- Winter jacket, hat, boots, gloves
- Sweaters
- Thick socks
- Skis (if you have them)

Plan well, and plan in advance, and guess what? Once you're there at your honeymoon destination, your poor planned-out body and mind won't have to plan anything else.

In other words, you'll be done with everything. So enjoy yourself. You'll have earned it.

Item	Description	Projected Cost*	Actual Cost*	Balance Due
TRANSPORTATION				
Airfare				
Car rental				
Moped rental				
Bike rental				
Train pass				
Taxi				
Parking fees				
Other				
ACCOMMODATIONS				
Wedding night				
Honeymoon destination				
Other				
FOOD				
Meal plan				
Meals				
Drinks				
ENTERTAINMENT				
SOUVENIRS				
SPENDING MONEY				
TIPS				
OTHER				
TOTAL				
* including tax, if applicable				

Travel Agency:

Name of travel agency: _____

Address: _____

_____

Telephone: _____ Fax number: _____

Contact: _____

Hours: _____

Directions: _____

_____

Car Rental Agency:

Name of car rental agency: _____

Address: _____

_____

Telephone: _____ Fax number: _____

Contact: _____

Hours: _____

Description of reserved vehicle (make/model): _____

_____

Terms: _____

Transportation:

Destination: _____

Carrier: _____ Flight/Route: _____

Departure date: _____ Time: _____

Arrival date: _____ Time: _____

Confirmation number: _____ Date: _____

Destination:

Carrier: | Flight/Route:

Departure date: | Time:

Arrival date: | Time:

Confirmation number: | Date:

Accommodations:

Hotel:

Address:

Directions:

Telephone: | Fax number:

Check-in date: | Time:

Check-out date: | Time:

Type of room:

Daily rate: | Total cost:

Confirmation number: | Date:

Hotel:

Address:

Directions:

Telephone: | Fax number:

Check-in date: | Time:

Check-out date: | Time:

Type of room:

Daily rate: | Total cost:

Confirmation number: | Date:

CHAPTER NINETEEN

LAST-MINUTE
DETAILS

Prewedding Checklist

Many of the following tasks may be (and probably should be) attended to in the days just before your wedding. Try to accomplish them all up to a week before the wedding. That way, you can relax and enjoy your last week of single life!

- ❧ Reconfirm plans with your officiant, reception site coordinator, photographer, videographer, band or DJ, florist, baker, limousine company, and hair stylist. Make sure they know the correct locations and times.
- ❧ Reconfirm your honeymoon travel arrangements and hotel reservations.
- ❧ Reconfirm your hotel reservation for your wedding night.
- ❧ Make sure your wedding attendants know where they need to be and when, and remind them of any special duties they need to perform.
- ❧ Finish any last-minute packing and review the Items to Remember Checklist in Chapter 19.
- ❧ Pack your going-away outfit and accessories. If you'll be changing at the reception site, put a trusted friend in charge of making sure they arrive there safely.
- ❧ Give your wedding rings and marriage license to your honor attendants to hold until the ceremony.
- ❧ Make sure your groom and best man have enough cash for tipping.
- ❧ Give an "emergency repair kit" (safety pins, extra hosiery, tissues, aspirin, etc.) to a trusted attendant, so you'll be better prepared to deal with the unexpected.
- ❧ Make sure your honeymoon luggage is stored in the trunk of your "getaway car" or is sent ahead to wherever you're spending your wedding night.
- ❧ Arrange for a friend to drive your car to the reception site if you intend to drive yourselves to the hotel or inn where you'll be staying.

Six to twelve months before the wedding:

- ❑ Announce engagement
- ❑ Decide on type of wedding
- ❑ Decide on time of day
- ❑ Choose the location
- ❑ Set a date
- ❑ Set a budget
- ❑ Select bridal party
- ❑ Plan color scheme
- ❑ Select and order bridal gown
- ❑ Select and order headpiece
- ❑ Select and order shoes
- ❑ Select and order attendants' gowns
- ❑ Start honeymoon planning
- ❑ Go to bridal gift registry
- ❑ Start compiling the guest list
- ❑ Select caterer
- ❑ Select musicians
- ❑ Select florist
- ❑ Select photographer
- ❑ Start planning reception
- ❑ Reserve hall, hotel, etc., for reception
- ❑ Plan to attend premarital counseling at your church, if applicable
- ❑ Select and order wedding rings

Three months before the wedding:

- ❑ Complete guest list
- ❑ Make doctor's appointments
- ❑ Plan to have mothers select attire
- ❑ Select and order invitations
- ❑ Order personal stationery
- ❑ Start compiling trousseau
- ❑ Finalize reception arrangements (rent items now)
- ❑ Make reservations for honeymoon
- ❑ Confirm dress delivery
- ❑ Confirm time and date with florist
- ❑ Confirm time and date with caterer
- ❑ Confirm time and date with photographer
- ❑ Confirm time and date with musicians
- ❑ Confirm time and date with church
- ❑ Discuss transportation to ceremony and reception
- ❑ Order cake
- ❑ Select and order attire for groomsmen
- ❑ Schedule bridesmaids' dress and shoe fittings

Two months before the wedding:

- ❏ Mail all invitations to allow time for RSVPs
- ❏ Arrange for appointment to get marriage license
- ❏ Finalize honeymoon arrangements

One month before the wedding:

- ❏ Schedule bridal portrait
- ❏ Reserve accommodations for guests
- ❏ Begin to record gifts received and send thank-you notes
- ❏ Plan rehearsal and rehearsal dinner
- ❏ Purchase gifts for bridal party
- ❏ Purchase gift for fiancé if gifts are being exchanged
- ❏ Schedule final fittings, including accessories and shoes
- ❏ Schedule appointments at beauty salon for attendants
- ❏ Schedule bridesmaids' luncheon or party
- ❏ Arrange for placement of guest book
- ❏ Obtain wedding props, e.g., pillow for ring bearer, candles, etc.
- ❏ Get marriage license

Two weeks before the wedding:

- ❏ Mail bridal portrait with announcement to newspaper
- ❏ Finalize wedding day transportation
- ❏ Arrange to change name on license, Social Security card, etc.
- ❏ Confirm accommodations for guests
- ❏ Prepare wedding announcements to be mailed after the wedding

One week before the wedding:

- ❏ Start packing for honeymoon
- ❏ Finalize number of guests with caterer
- ❏ Double-check all details with those providing professional services (photographer, videographer, florist, etc.)
- ❏ Plan seating arrangements
- ❏ Confirm desired pictures with photographer
- ❏ Style your hair with headpiece
- ❏ Practice applying cosmetics in proper light
- ❏ Arrange for one last fitting of all wedding attire
- ❏ Make sure rings are picked up and fit properly

- ❏ Confirm receipt of marriage license
- ❏ Have rehearsal/rehearsal dinner (one or two days before wedding)
- ❏ Arrange to have the photographer and attendants arrive two hours before ceremony if there are to be prewedding pictures
- ❏ Arrange for music to start one half hour prior to ceremony
- ❏ Arrange to have the mother of the groom seated five minutes before ceremony

- ❏ Arrange to have the mother of the bride seated immediately before the processional
- ❏ Arrange for the aisle runner to be rolled out by the ushers immediately before the processional

On your wedding day:

- ❏ Try to relax and pamper yourself; take a long bath, have a manicure, etc.
- ❏ Eat at least one small meal
- ❏ Have your hair and makeup done a few hours before ceremony
- ❏ Start dressing one to two hours before ceremony

Bride:

Name:

Address:

Telephone:

Groom:

Name:

Address:

Telephone:

Family Members:

Name:

Address:

Telephone:

Name:

Address:

Telephone:

Name:

Address:

Telephone:

Name:

Address:

Telephone:

Wedding Party Members:

Name:

Address:

Telephone:

Name:

Address:

Telephone:

Name:

Address:

Telephone:

Name:

Address:

Telephone:

Name: _____

Address: _____

_____

Telephone: _____

Name: _____

Address: _____

_____

Telephone: _____

Name: _____

Address: _____

_____

Telephone: _____

Name: _____

Address: _____

_____

Telephone: _____

Wedding Consultant:

Name: _____

Address: _____

_____

Telephone: _____

Ceremony Officiant and Site:

Name: _____

Address: _____

_____

Telephone: _____

Reception Coordinator and Site:

Name: _____

Address: _____

_____

Telephone: _____

Jeweler:

Name: _____

Address: _____

_____

Telephone: _____

Bridal Salon:

Name: _____

Address: _____

_____

Telephone: _____

_____

Men's Formalwear Shop:

Name:

Address:

Telephone:

Caterer:

Name:

Address:

Telephone:

Baker:

Name:

Address:

Telephone:

Equipment Rental Company:

Name:

Address:

Telephone:

Photographer:

Name:

Address:

Telephone:

Videographer:

Name:

Address:

Telephone:

Band, DJ, and Other Musicians:

Name:

Address:

Telephone:

Name:

Address:

Telephone:

Limousine Service:

Name:

Address:

Telephone:

Travel Agent:

Name:

Address:

Telephone: